Cambridge ICT Starters

Next Steps Stage 2

Third Edition

Jill Jesson and Graham Peacock

AF823051

CAMBRIDGE
UNIVERSITY PRESS

CAMBRIDGE
UNIVERSITY PRESS

University Printing House, Cambridge CB2 8BS, United Kingdom

Cambridge University Press is part of the University of Cambridge.

It furthers the University's mission by disseminating knowledge in the pursuit of education, learning and research at the highest international levels of excellence.

Information on this title: education.cambridge.org

First published 2003
Second edition 2005
Third edition 2013
3rd printing 2015

Printed in Poland by Opolgraf

A catalogue record for this publication is available from the British Library

ISBN 978-1-107-62513-6 Paperback

Additional resources for this publication at www.cambridgeindia.org

Introduction

Cambridge ICT Starters: Next Steps, Stage 2 has been written to support learners who are following the Cambridge ICT Starters syllabus. It follows the syllabus closely and provides full coverage of all the modules. The sections of the book correspond to the modules and follow the order in which the modules appear in the syllabus. The book builds on writing and modifying commands to produce pictures and designs; searching, retrieving and storing internet information; setting up and managing an email account in order to compose, edit, read and respond to emails; and creating and organising multimedia presentations.

The book provides learners and their helpers with:

- examples of activities to do
- exercises for practice
- instruction in using their computers
- optional extension and challenge activities

It is designed for use in the classroom with coaching from trained teachers. Where possible the work has been set in real situations where the computer will be of direct use. The activities are fairly sophisticated yet simple enough to be followed by adults as well as children!

Some exercises require the learners to open prepared files for editing. These files are available to teachers on www.cambridgeindia.org website. The website provides useful graphics and templates for creating pictograms. Some pictures and text files are also included to help young learners so that they can learn editing without first creating the files required.

The activities in this book use Windows 7, Microsoft Office 2007 software, Microsoft Outlook Express 2007, Microsoft Internet Explorer and MSWLogo. However, the syllabus does not specify any particular type of software in order to meet the learning objectives.

Please note that when learners view the screen shots contained in this book on their computer screens, all the type will be clearly legible.

Contents

NEXT STEPS: Stage 2

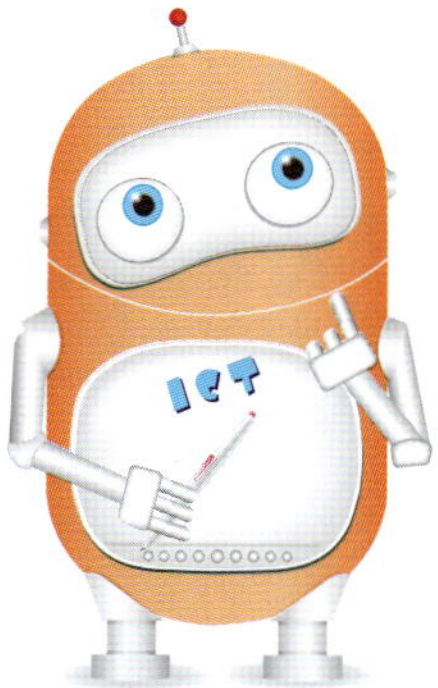

Module 5
Exploring Control

Learning Objectives

	Student is able to:	Pass/ Merit
1	Write a list of commands to produce a simple picture or design	P
2	Use repeat commands	P
3	Create complex shapes with varied angles	M
4	Name and run a procedure	M

5.1 Exploring control

Learning Objective: 1

MSWLogo

- Click to open the Start menu.
- Click All Programs.
- Click Microsoft Windows Logo.
- Use the commander to give instructions to the screen turtle.
- After typing each command, tap Enter to execute the command.
    - To make the turtle move forward 100 units, type fd 100.
    - To make the turtle move forward 77 units, type fd 77.
    - To make the turtle turn 90° to the right, type rt 90.
    - To make the turtle turn 45° to the left, type lt 45.

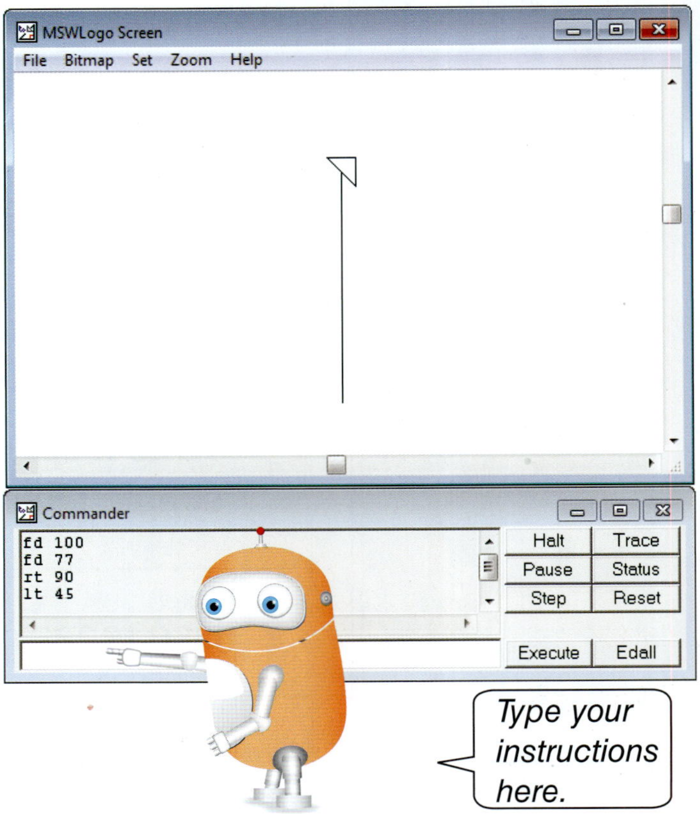

Penup and pendown

- Click Reset to start a new blank page.
- Type: fd 30
  penup
- Type: fd 30
  pendown
- Type: fd 50
  penup
  fd 10
  pendown
  fd 20
- Type: CT
  CT will clear all the texts in the commander box.
- Type: CS
  CS will clear the screen. It has the same effect as Reset.

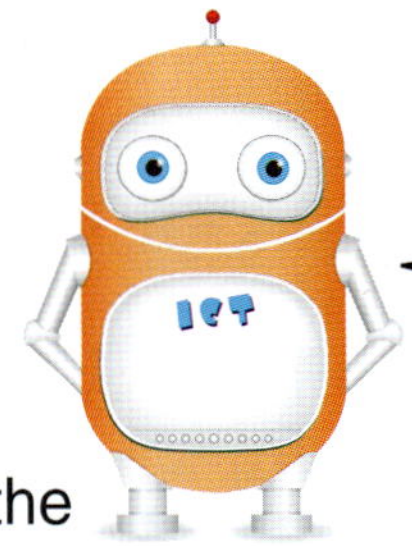

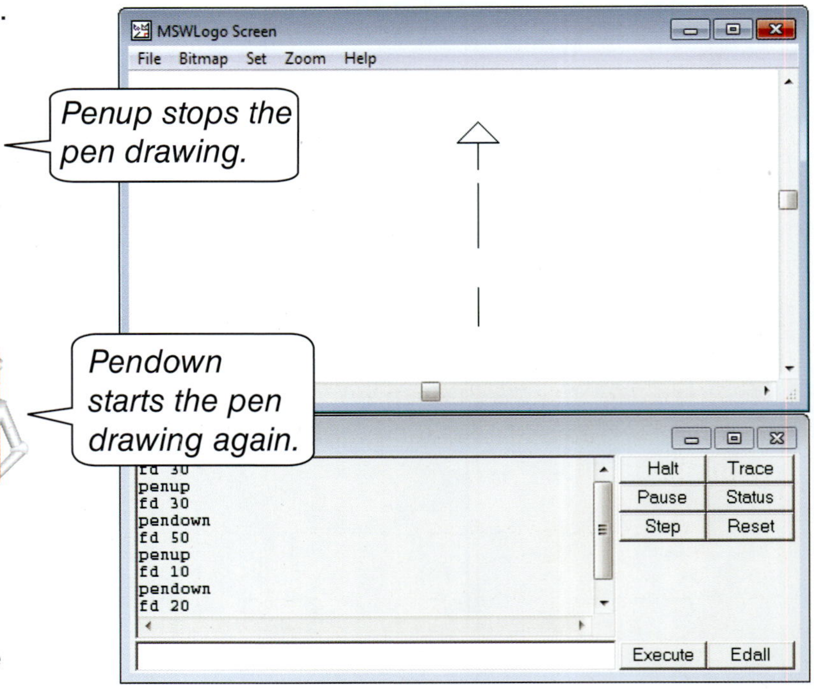

Square

- Type the following list of commands to draw a square with sides of 100 units:
  - fd 100 rt 90
  - fd 100 rt 90
  - fd 100 rt 90
  - fd l00 rt 90

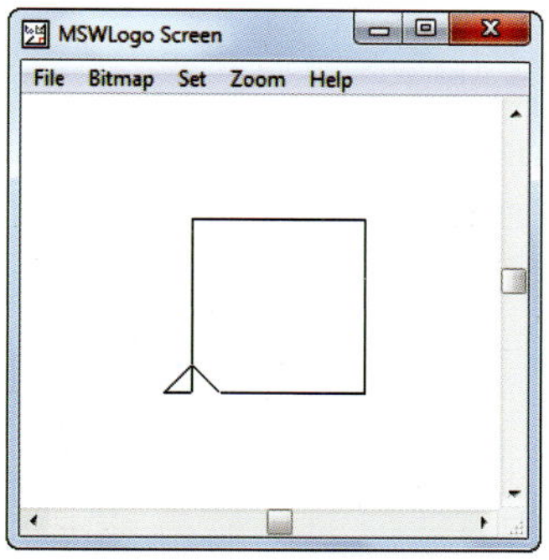

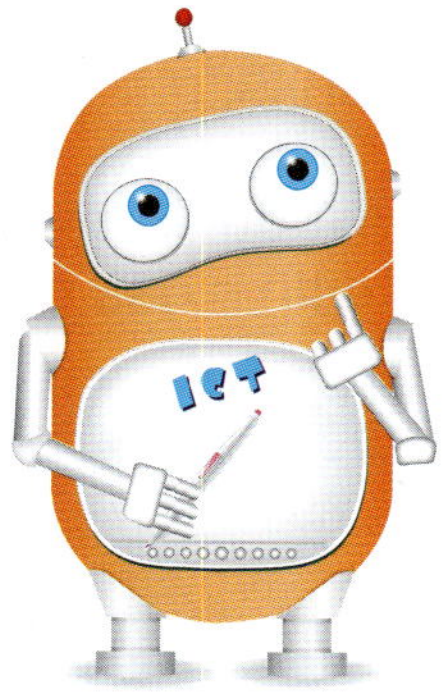

- Type the command penup.
- Move your turtle to a new position using the fd command.
- Type the command pendown.
- Draw another square with sides of 150 units.
- Write down the list of commands that you used to create the new square:

____

____

____

____

____

Rectangle

- Type the following list of commands to draw a rectangle with width 100 and length 150 units:
  - fd l00 rt 90
  - fd l50 rt 90
  - fd 100 rt 90
  - fd l50 rt 90

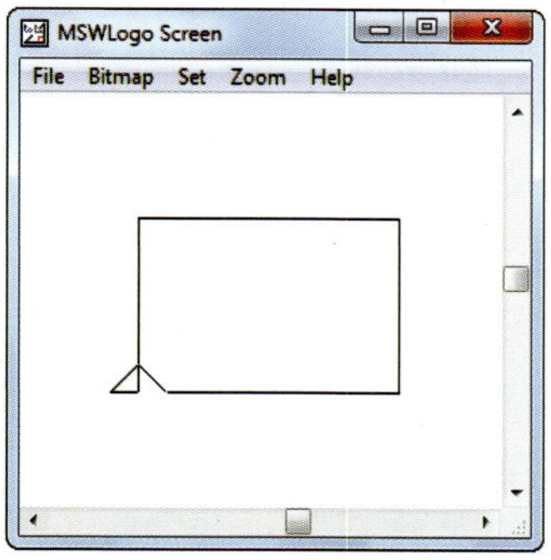

- Type the command penup.
- Move your turtle to a new position using the fd command.
- Type the command pendown.
- Draw another rectangle with width 70 and length 170 units. Write the list of commands you used:

____

____

____

____

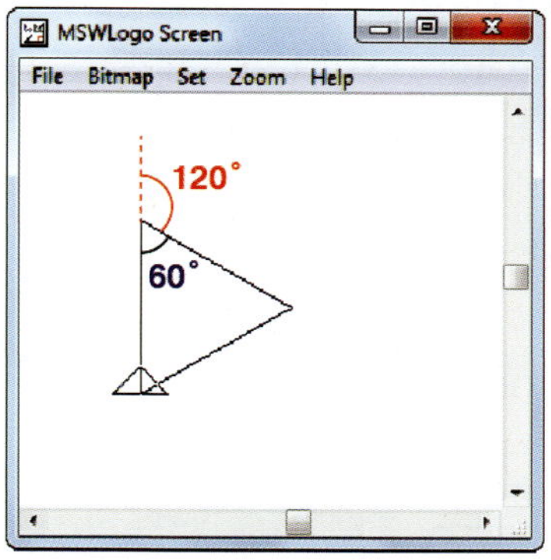

- Discuss and write down how you would draw a regular triangle with each side 130 units and each interior angle 60° (i.e. exterior angle 120°):

____

____

____

____

____

____

5.2 Turtle repeats

Learning Objective: 2

Use repeat for drawing triangles, squares and rectangles

- You can use the repeat command to save time typing repeated commands when drawing triangles, squares and rectangles.
- To draw a regular triangle with sides of 75 units and exterior angle 120°, instead of typing fd 75 rt 120 3 times, you can type: repeat 3 [fd 75 rt 120]
- Execute the commands to test whether you have got the right shape.
- Change your commands for drawing 3 regular triangles with sides of 100, 150 and 250 units.
- Complete the commands below for drawing a square with sides of 100 units: repeat ___ [fd ______]
- Change the commands for squares with sides of 70, 90 and 120 units.
- Complete the commands below for drawing a rectangle with width 45 units and length 70 units: repeat___[fd______fd______]
- Change the commands to draw a rectangle with sides of 90 and 145 units.

Polygons

- Polygons are shapes with more than 4 sides.
- A regular hexagon has 6 equal sides and 6 equal exterior angles of 60°.
- To draw a regular hexagon with sides of 100 units, you need to type fd 100 rt 60 6 times.
- By using the repeat command you only need to type repeat 6 [fd 100 rt 60].
- Execute the commands.
- Do you get a regular hexagon?

Make sure you leave a space between repeat and 6. Use square brackets only!

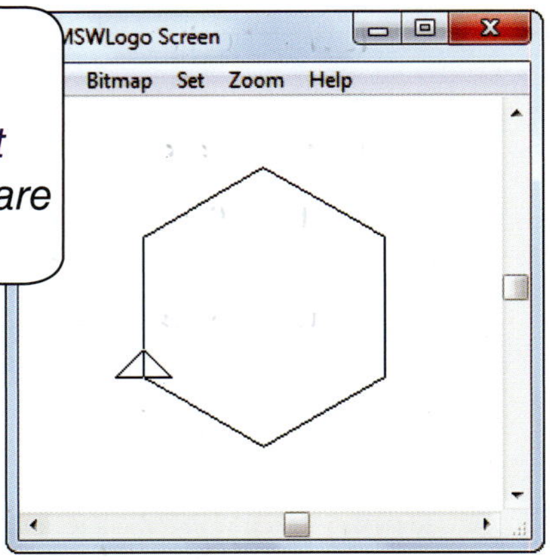

More polygons

- Complete the commands below to draw a regular pentagon with each side 70 units and each exterior angle 72°: repeat____ [________________]
- Write the commands using repeat to draw a regular octagon with each side 70 units and each exterior angle 45°:

____

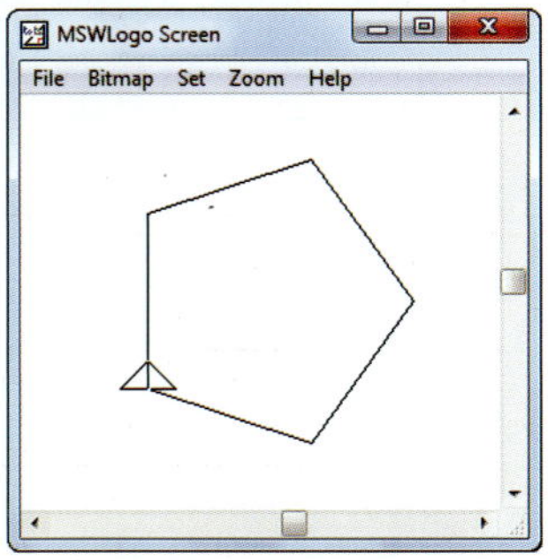

A pentagon has 5 sides and an octagon has 8 sides.

The exterior angle of a polygon = 360°/n, where n is the number of sides.

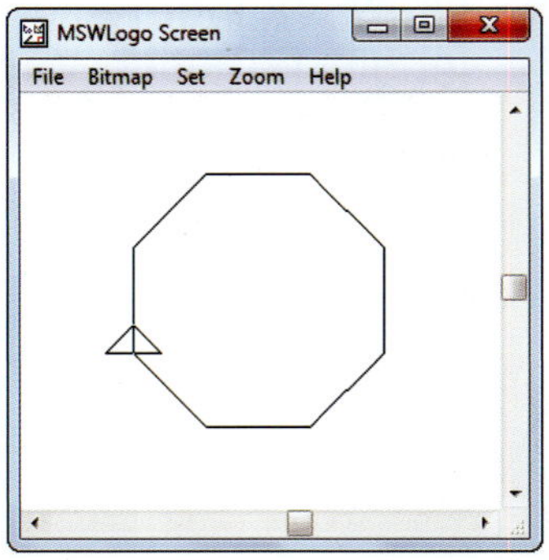

Patterns with varied angles

- Type the following list of commands to draw the letter A. Tap Enter at the end of each line.
  - rt 30 fd 180
  - rt 120 fd 180
  - bk 70 rt 120 fd 110

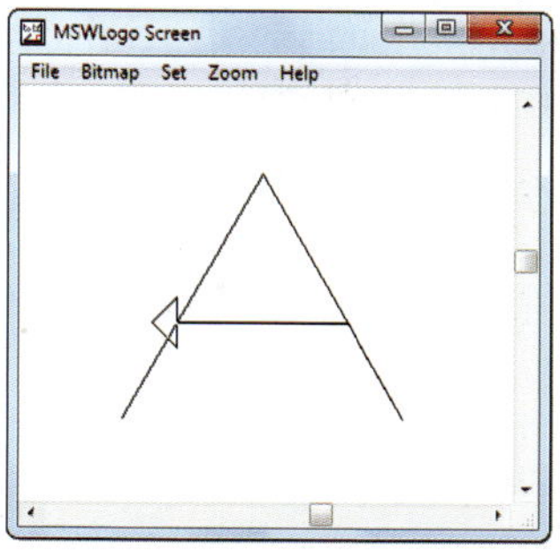

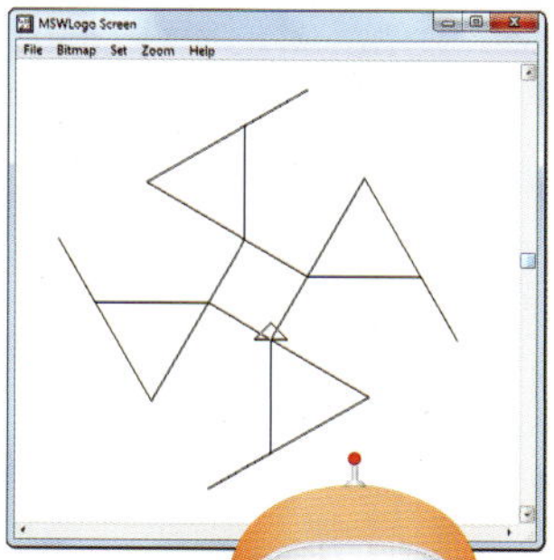

- Starting from the ending position of the turtle, type the list of commands another 3 times to form a flower pattern.

The pattern depends on the starting and ending positions. You may have a different pattern if your starting and ending positions are different.

Letters K and M

- Write down the list of commands for forming the letter K (or any other letter that you like).
- You can use the sample as a guide or create your own picture.
- Test your list of commands.
- Change the list of commands when and where necessary.

  List of commands for K:

  ____

  ____

  ____

  ____

  ____

  ____

  ____

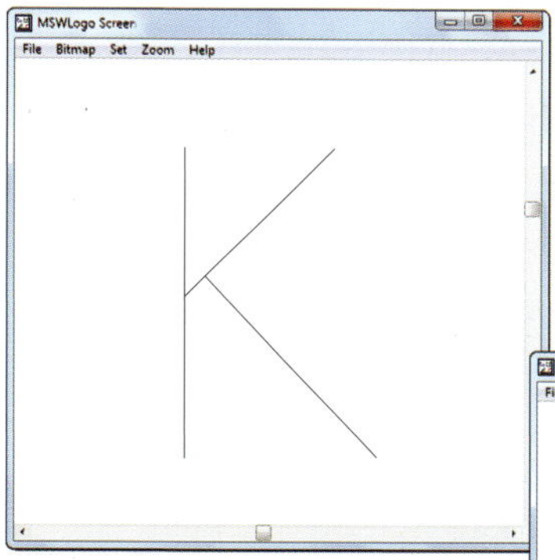

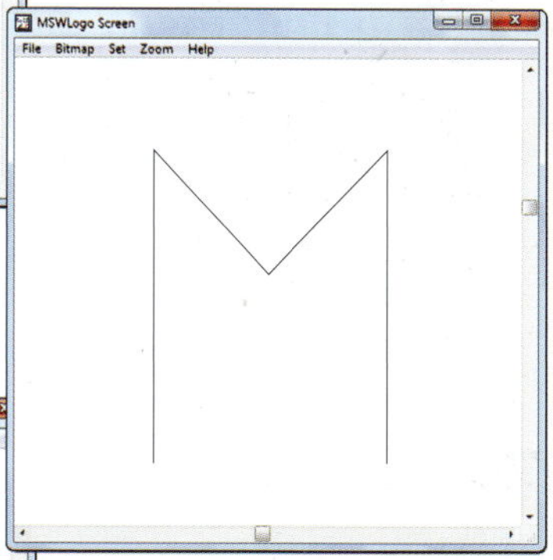

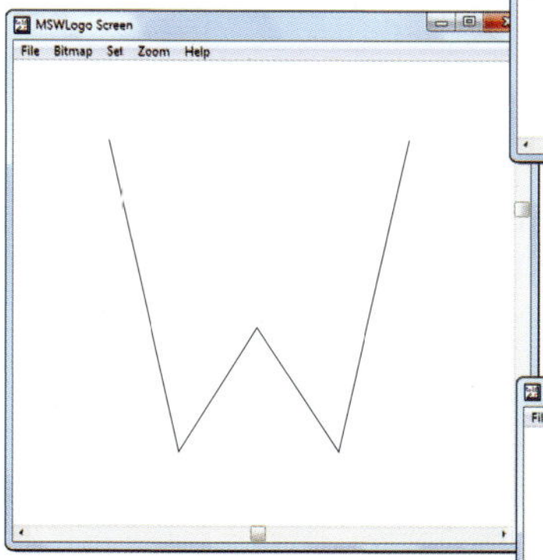

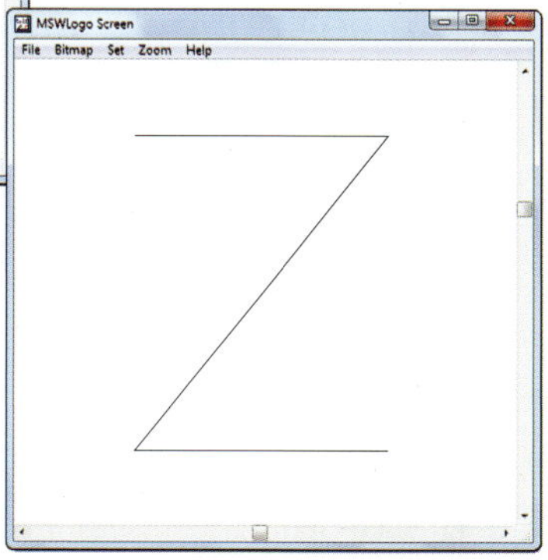

- When you have completed the picture, do a screenshot of your work and save it as an MS Word document.
- Print a copy of the image and glue it in your exercise book.
- Repeat for 3 more letters, M, W and Z, or any letters of your choice.

Patterns by rotation

- Type and execute the following commands:
  repeat 3 [rt 120 fd 75] rt 45
- Execute the above commands 8 times and finally type: ht

The command ht will hide the turtle so that the pattern is clearer. To see the turtle again, type st (show turtle).

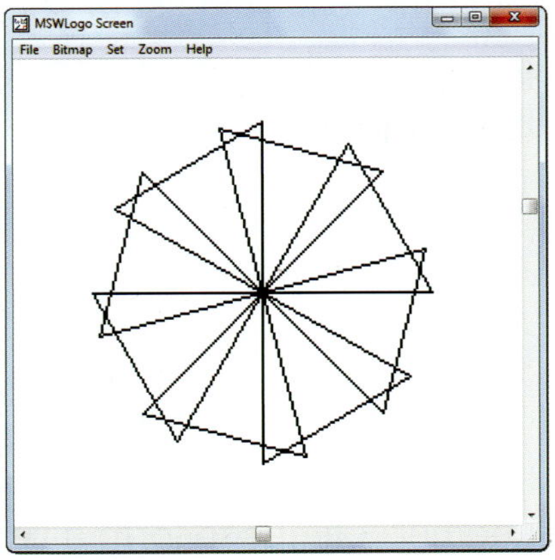

More patterns

- Start a new drawing.
- Type CT CS to clear the text in the commander and to clear the screen.
- At the commander type:
  repeat 8 [repeat 4 [rt 90 fd 75] rt 45] ht
- You are actually repeating the drawing of a square (repeat 4 [rt 90 fd 75]) 8 times, but the turtle turns to the right 45° after drawing each square.
- Change the angle 45° to 20°, 30°, 60° etc. to create different patterns.
- You need to change the number of times the patterns are repeated in order to make complete patterns.

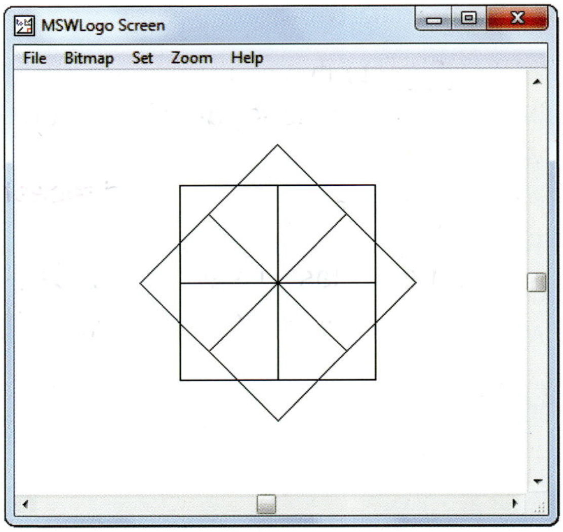

Flower patterns

- Type CT CS to clear the text in the commander and to clear the screen.
- Create your own flower patterns by completing the blanks below with appropriate numbers:
  repeat__[repeat__[rt__fd__] rt___]
- The command in blue can be a triangle, a square, a rectangle. You can also try a regular pentagon, a hexagon or an octagon.
- Test your command.
- Do a screenshot and save it as an MS Word document.
- Print a copy and glue it in your exercise book.

Glue your flower pattern in your exercise book.

5.5 Writing procedures

Learning Objective: 4

Procedures

Make a square procedure

- Click File.
- Select Edit... .
- Type square on the first row as the name of the procedure.
- Click OK to open the Editor.
- Place the cursor on the right side of the procedure name: to square.
- Tap ↵Enter to insert a line.
- Type the command for drawing a square:
  repeat 4 [fd 55 rt 90]
- You can highlight the command repeat 4 [fd 55 rt 90] and click Test! to test the command.
- Make sure the last line end is not deleted.
- Click File under the Editor mode.
- Click Save and Exit .
- Type CT CS to clear the text in the commander and to clear the screen.
- To draw the square, just type at the commander:
  square and tap ↵Enter to execute.

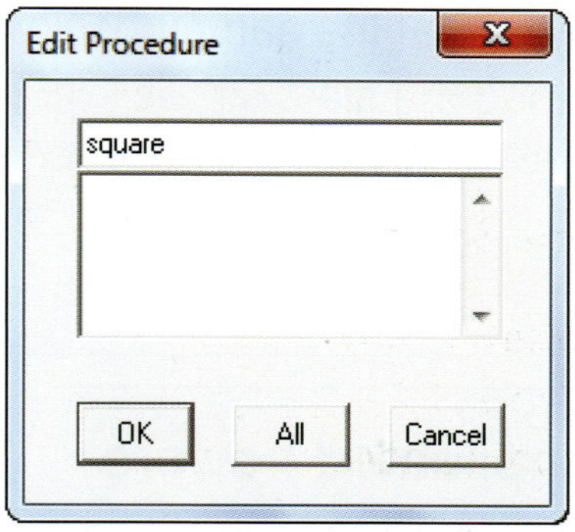

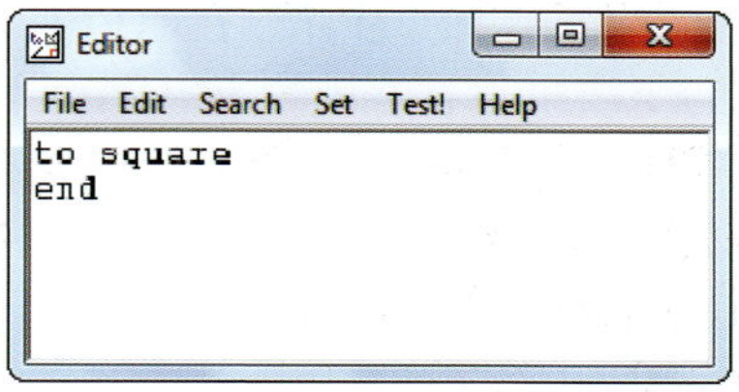

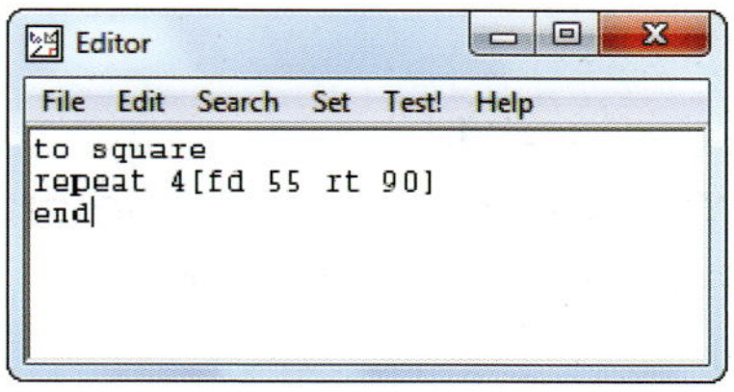

Procedure for shapes

- Repeat the previous exercise to create a procedure to draw a triangle.
- Create another procedure for drawing a regular pentagon, a regular hexagon and a regular octagon. Creating a procedure is called defining one.
- Before you leave Logo, save your file to keep the procedures.
- Click File.
- Click SaveAs... .
- Save your file as exercise1.lgo.
- You must load exercise1.lgo the next time you start Logo in order to use the procedures.

5.6 Repeat a procedure

Learning Objectives: 2, 4

Flower patterns

- You can tell the computer to repeat a procedure.
- If, after drawing the picture, your ending position is back to the starting position, you must tell the turtle to turn or move forward after drawing the first shape.
- Otherwise, if you use the repeat command to draw the shape many times, the turtle will only draw the same shape over and over again, at the same position.
- Load the file exercise1.lgo that you have saved in your previous exercise.
- Type at the commander:
  repeat 20 [triangle rt 18]
- Do the same by repeating a square, a hexagon, a pentagon and an octagon.

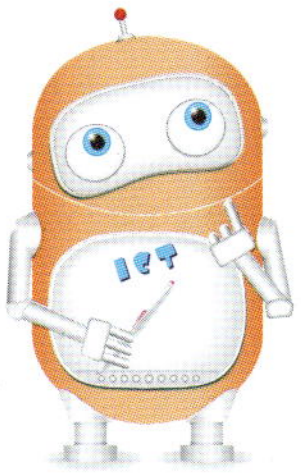

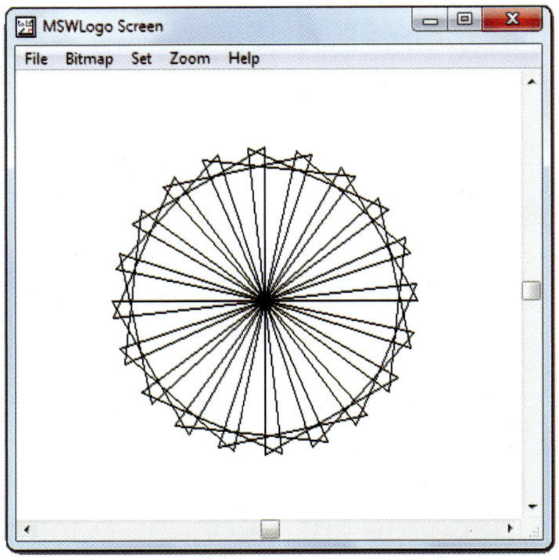

Complicated flowers

- You can make more complicated flowers by adding a slight forward movement, more repeats and different amounts of turns.
- Here is an example:
  - First define procedure square as
    repeat 4 [fd 55 rt 90]
  - At the commander type:
    repeat 20 [square rt 20 fd 10]

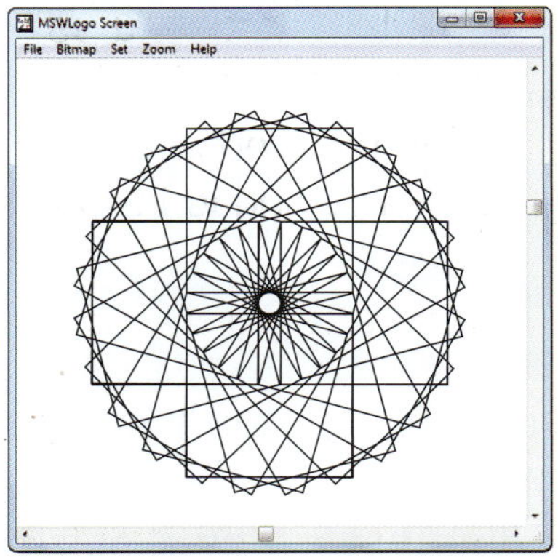

Mystery

- What shape do you think the procedure mystery below will create?
  lt 45 fd 30 rt 135 fd 10 lt 90 fd 40
  rt 90 fd 22 rt 90 fd 40 lt 90 fd 10
  rt 135 fd 30 rt 135
- Define the procedure mystery and find out what it is.
- Clear the screen.
- At the commander type:
  penup home pendown
  repeat 8 [mystery rt 45]
- Do a screenshot of the picture created and save it as an MS Word document flower1.
- Try another two patterns:
  repeat 30 [mystery rt 20]
  repeat 30 [mystery rt 20 fd 10]
- Start each pattern as a new bitmap.
- Do a screenshot of each pattern created and save them as pattern2, pattern3 respectively.
- Save the procedure as mystery.lgo.

Letter pattern

- Refer back to the lists of commands for creating letters in exercise 5.3.
- You can create new lists of commands if you have not saved them.
- Define the procedure letter_Z for creating the letter Z.
- Leave the ending position as it is.
- Save the procedure as letter.lgo.
- Use the repeat command to create a flower pattern.
- Example:
  repeat 4[letter_z]

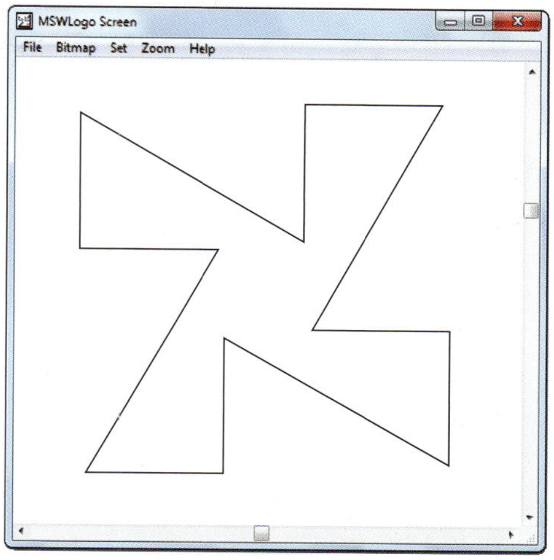

More letter patterns

- Define more procedures for creating letters.
- Save all these procedures under the same file letter.lgo.
- Use these procedures and the repeat command to form more patterns.
- The samples shown here are patterns formed by letters G, K and C.

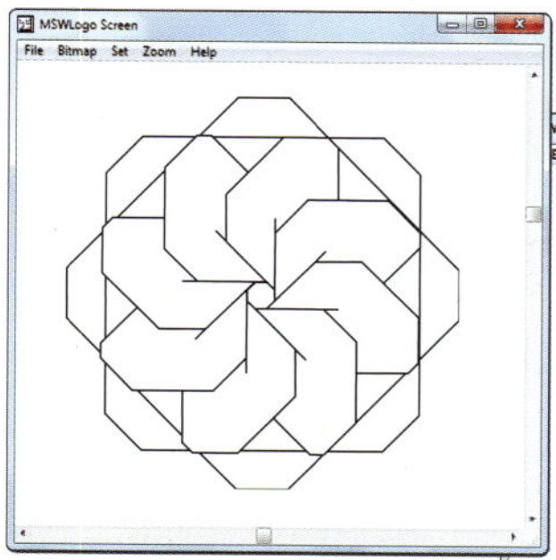
Pattern formed by letter G

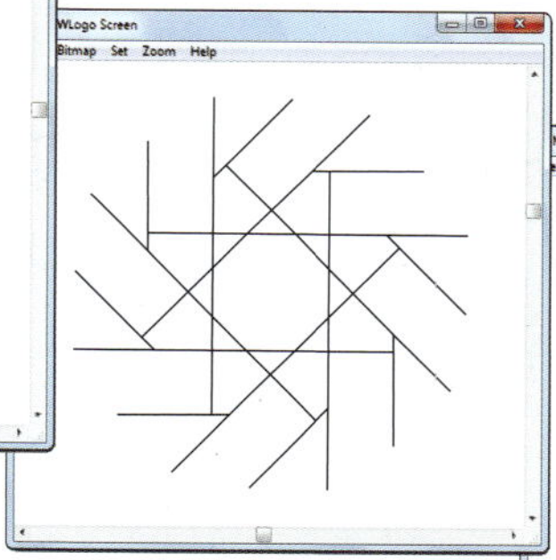
Pattern formed by letter K

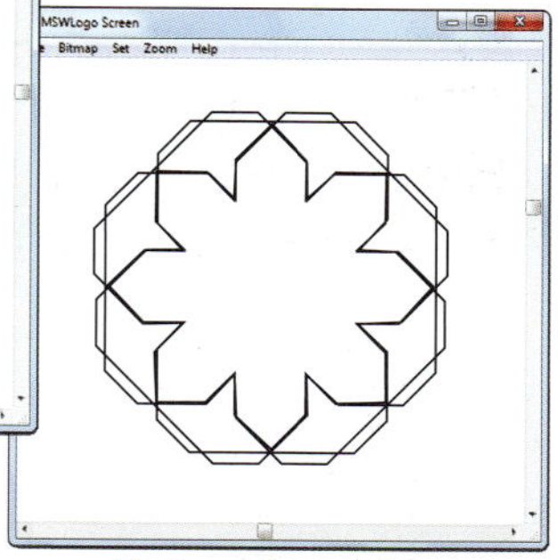
Pattern formed by letter C

Project

- Create a procedure flag to produce the flag as shown.
- Save the procedure as flag.lgo.
- Maximise the Editor window.
- Do a screenshot to capture the list of commands that you used to define the procedure flag.
- Save the capture as an MS Word document pro_flag.
- Use the flag procedure to produce a complicated pattern.
- Do a screenshot and save it as an MS Word document FlagPattern.

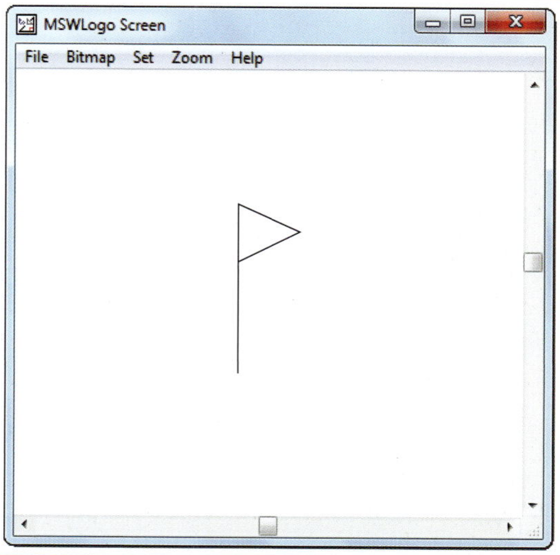

Optional extension and challenge activities

Module 5 – Exploring Control

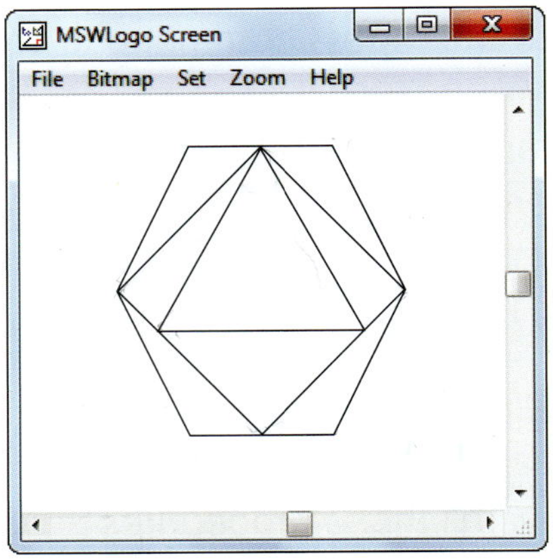

Challenge 1

Use penup and pendown to draw a triangle inside a square inside a hexagon.

Challenge 2

- List the commands to draw a pentagon.
- Make a rotating pattern by programming the turtle to draw the pentagon 5 times using the repeat command and turning 72° after each repeat.

Challenge 3

- Define the procedure for creating a letter of your choice with the turtle.
- Save the procedure.
- Use the procedure and the repeat command to create a rotating pattern.

Module 6
Exploring the Internet

Learning Objectives

	Student is able to:	Pass/ Merit
1	Use Internet tools to find information	P
2	Evaluate relevance and usefulness of material	P
3	Store and retrieve information	P
4	Copy and paste information from a website	P
5	Save URLs and objects from a website	M
6	Use extended search skills	M

The links

- The Internet started out as an international network of computers (shortened to Internet). The heart of the Internet is computers all round the world which are permanently linked together by high-speed telephones. You link to the Internet by hooking your home or school computer to one of these linked computers.

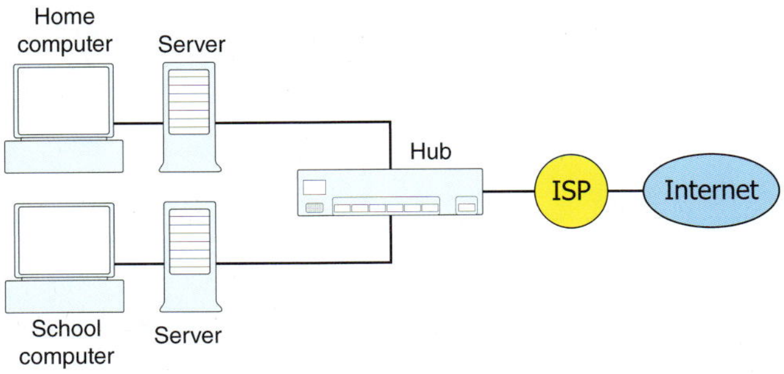

- Your computer is linked to the heart of the Internet by companies called Internet Service Providers (ISP). Some provide many features and charge you to use this service. Others do not charge directly for the service.
- The World Wide Web (WWW) is a store of information on web pages which you can see through the Internet.
- Pages on the web are linked by hyperlinks. These are texts or pictures which make links between pages on the web. Links are often coloured. They change colour when you click on them.

Languages

- People transfer web pages using a computer language called Hypertext Transfer Protocol (HTTP).
- People transfer files across the Internet using a computer language called File Transfer Protocol (FTP). If you want to download a file of information from a website, your browser (e.g. Netscape, Internet Explorer, etc.) will automatically use FTP.
- People write web pages in a computer language called Hypertext Mark-up Language (HTML).

Finding the sites

- Each site on the WWW has an address. This is in the form of a Uniform Resource Locator (URL).
- For example, the URL of the Natural History Museum in London is www.nhm.ac.uk.
- To go to a site, type the URL in the address box and tap ↵ Enter.
- On the other hand, if you are not sure where the information is, you need a search engine.
- Search engines, e.g. www.MSN.com, www.google.com, www.yahoo.com, are sites which find other sites on the web.
- In order to come back to the same website, you can add it to your favourites folder.

Test yourself

Fill in the blanks.

- Replace _____ with missing initials.
- Replace .... with missing words.

I wanted to read web pages on the .... To do this, I used an ________ to link my computer to the web. I typed in the ________ of a site I knew and went straight there. I clicked on the coloured .... which took me from page to page. On one page, I downloaded a file using ________. I needed more information about a shop in my city, so I used a .... called Google to find it. To remember the address of the site, I saved it in my .... folder.

Remember the basic rules of Internet safety: do not give your address or phone numbers to people who are not known to you or your parents or guardians.

6.2 Browsing web pages

Internet Explorer

- Click to open Start menu.
- Click **All Programs**.
- Click **Internet Explorer**.
- A home page is shown. The home page depends on the setting for Internet options of the computer that you are using.
- To view a different web page, at the space provided for Web Search type the URL that you wish to visit, e.g. http://www.cambridgeindia.org
- Click or tap **Enter**.

Sue

- Type fieldmuseum.org into the URL box.
- Type AT Rex named sue in the search box given on the museum's web page and press **Enter** or click on .
- Click the orange link.

Who is Sue?

- Find out three interesting facts about Sue and write them here.

....

....

....

....

....

....

....

More about Sue

- Use Google Search and key words to find out more about Sue.
- Can you find the following information?

Age: ___ million years.

Length: ___ feet (___ metres)

Height at hips: ___ feet (___ metres)

Estimated live weight: ___ tons (___ metric tons)

Weight of skull: ___ pounds (___ kg)

Length of skull: ___ feet (___ metres)

Is Sue a male or female T. rex? Find out.

Kids Yahoo

- Type the URL: http://kids.yahoo.com/
- Tap [Enter] to go into the page.
- Click on a link which interests you, e.g. STUDYZONE.
- Follow the links to find three interesting facts about the chosen topic.
- Open a new blank MS Word document to record the URL and the information from this website.

Copying the URL

- Highlight the URL.
- Hold [Ctrl] down and tap [C] for copy.
- Switch to MS Word.
- Click [Paste] or hold [Ctrl] and tap [V].

Copying graphics

- To copy the graphic, place the mouse pointer on top of the graphic.
- Right-click the mouse button to trigger the shortcut menu.
- Select Copy Image .
- Switch over to MS Word.
- Click .

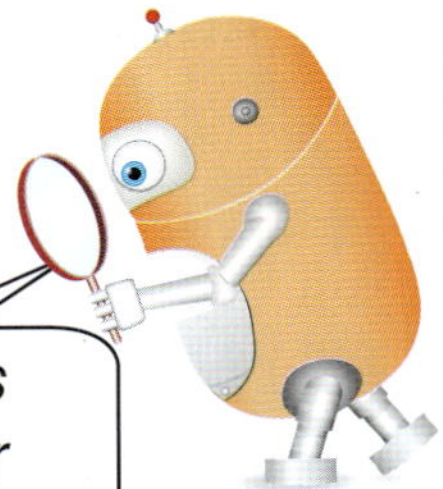

Only copy graphics from the Internet for private use or you may break copyright rules.

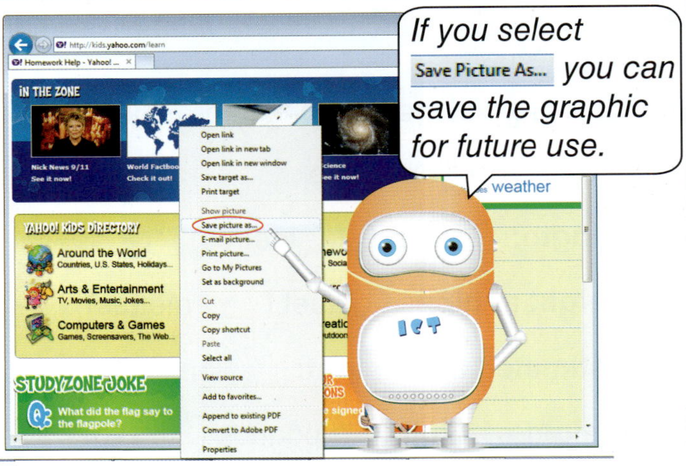

If you select Save Picture As... you can save the graphic for future use.

Copying text

- Highlight the text that you wish to copy.
- You can include the graphic and caption.
- Hold Ctrl down and tap C for copy.
- Switch over to MS Word.
- Click .
- Save the document with an appropriate file name.
- When you have copied three different facts, use the edit tools to rewrite them in your own words.
- Save after each paste or alteration to the text.
- Save your final copy.

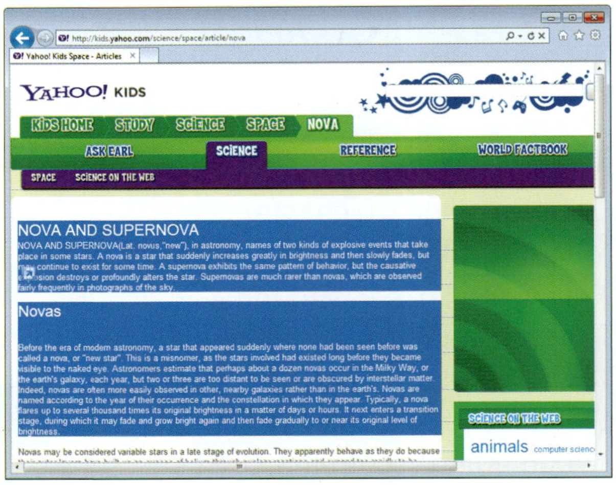

NOVA AND SUPERNOVA

NOVA AND SUPERNOVA(Lat. novus,"new"), in astronomy, names of two kinds of explosive events that take place in some stars. A nova is a star that suddenly increases greatly in brightness and then slowly fades, but may continue to exist for some time. A supernova exhibits the same pattern of behavior, but the causative explosion destroys or profoundly alters the star. Supernovas are much rarer than novas, which are observed fairly frequently in photographs of the sky.

Novas

Novas may be considered variable stars in a late stage of evolution. They apparently behave as they do because their outer layers have built up an excess of helium through nuclear reactions and expand too rapidly to be contained. The star explosively emits a small fraction of its mass as a shell of gas--the cause of the increase in brightnes--and then settles down. Such a star is typically a white dwarf and is commonly thought to be the smaller member of a binary (two-star) system, subject to a continuous infall of matter from the larger star. This is perhaps always the case with dwarf novas, which erupt repeatedly at regular intervals of a few to hundreds of days.

Supernovas

A supernova explosion is far more spectacular and destructive than a nova and much rarer. Such events may occur no more than once every few years in the Galaxy; and despite their increase in brilliance by a factor of billions, only a few are ever observable to the naked eye. Until 1987, only three had been positively identified in recorded history, the best known of which is the one that occurred in ad 1054 and is now known as the Crab nebula. Supernovas, like novas, are more often seen in other galaxies.

Here is some information that I copied about Supernovas.

Learning Objectives: 1, 3

Search engine

- Type the URL address: www.google.com and tap ↵Enter to start the search engine Google.
- To find information about volcanoes, type volcanoes and click Google Search .
- A list of search results will be shown.

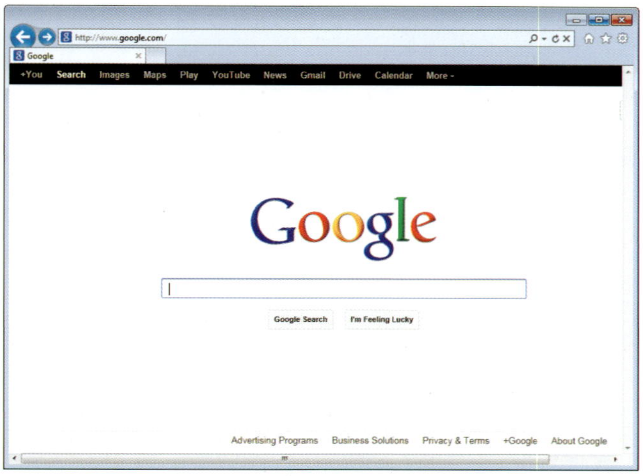

Search results

- A list of websites about volcanoes will be displayed.
- Read the descriptions carefully and select the one that suits your need.
- To go to the website chosen, click on the title line, e.g. **volcanoes**.

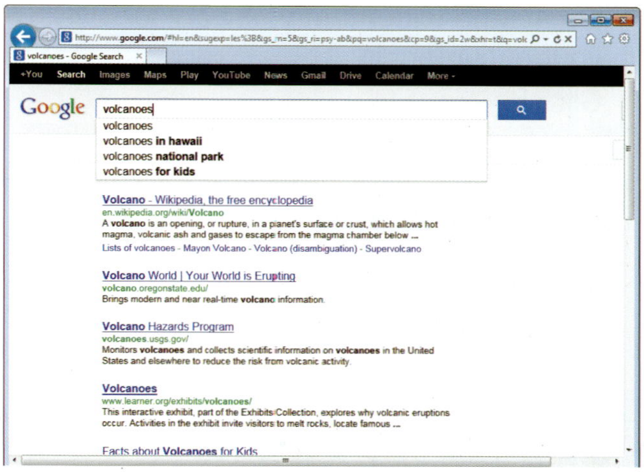

Bookmark

- In order to come back to the same website, you can add the website to your Favourites folder.
- Click ☆ to add the page to your favourites list.
- The Favourites folder will be displayed.
- Click Add to favorites... to get the following dialogue box.

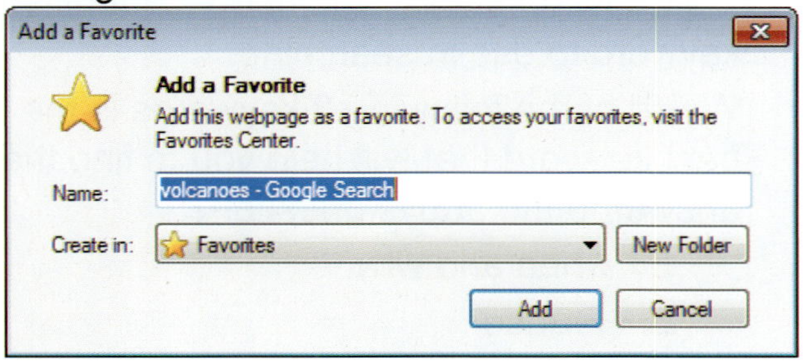

- Check the name to see whether it is correct.
- Click Add if it is correct and the website is added to the list.

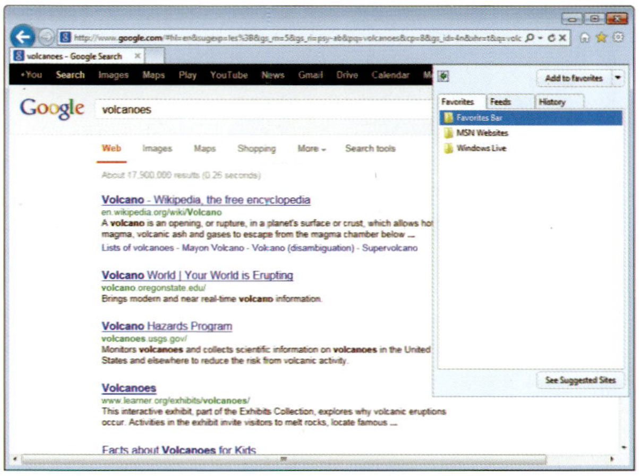

Saving the page

- Bookmark only saves the URL, but you can save the whole web page and view it again when you are offline!
- Click the Page ▾ button, and then click Save as... .
- To save all the information as a single file select Web Archive, single file(*.mht).
- Locate the folder that you want to save your document in.
- Click Save .

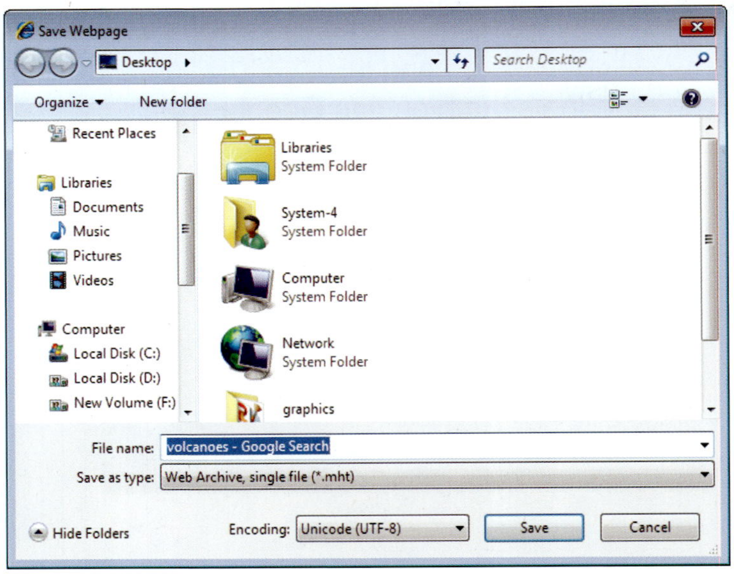

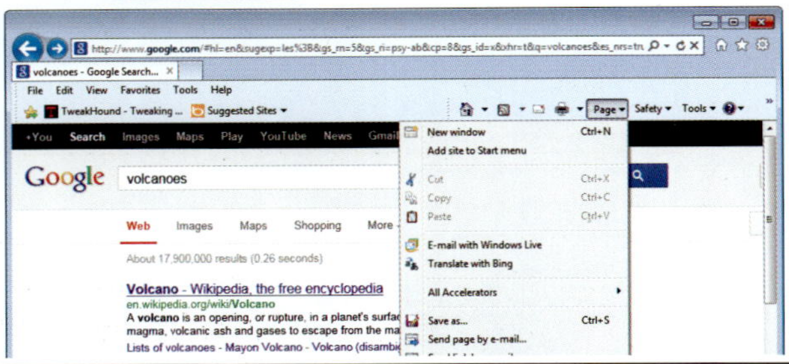

Open saved web page

- You can open the web page when you are offline.
- Locate the file that you have saved.
- Click volcanoes - Google Search .

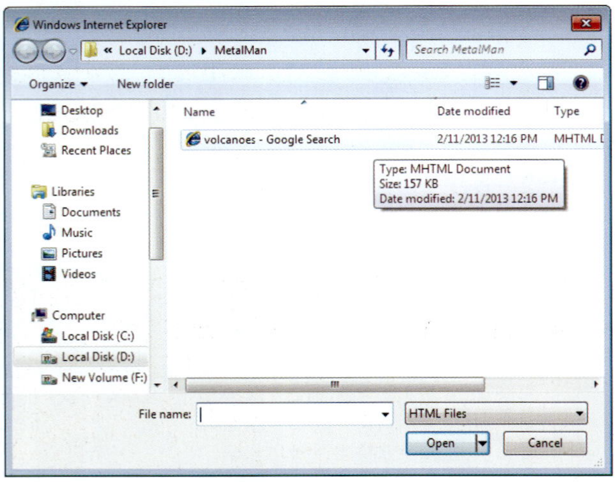

Extended search

- When and why was the Eiffel Tower of France built?

- Before you can obtain information to answer the question above, you need to identify the keyword to use in searching.
- Which of the following 3 keywords is the best keyword that will help you to find the answer to the above question?
  1. when and why
  2. France
  3. Eiffel Tower

Evaluate search results

- Use the keywords that you have identified and the Google search engine to search for the answer.
- Open a blank Word document to record your search results and evaluation of the search results.
- Type the first keyword ________________ (refer to page 17) to search.
- From the list of search results, select at least 3 websites.
- Type the question When and why was the Eiffel Tower of France built? as the heading of your Word document.
- Go to the websites selected.
- Copy each of the URLs and paste it in the Word document under the subheading Websites visited.
- Write a short comment about what the links contain in relation to the search topic.
- Compare all the websites that you visited under this search and state which of these sites contains the best information in relation to the search topic.
- Save your Word document as Eiffel Tower.

Gawai Dayak

- Gawai Dayak is a very special occasion in Sarawak, the largest state in Malaysia. Find out from the Internet 'How is the festival Gawai Dayak celebrated in Sarawak?'
- Open a blank Word document to record your findings.
- Use the Google search engine to find out about the festival.
- Write down in the Word document the keyword that you would use to start the search.
- From the search results, pick and visit at least 5 websites to find the answer.
- Select 2 paragraphs that best describe the festival.
- Copy and paste the paragraphs in the same document.
- Copy a festival-related photograph and paste it together with the paragraphs of text.
- Select and copy 3 URLs that you think are most useful in searching for information about Gawai Dayak.
- Write a brief comment about each link in relation to Gawai Dayak.
- Pick and explain which website is the best one in relation to the information about Gawai Dayak.
- Save your document as Gawai Dayak.

Optional extension and challenge activities

Module 6 – Exploring the Internet

Challenge 1

- Find a website which gives you information about a local zoo or museum.
- Copy pictures of some exhibits which interest you.
- Add text, and a map of how to get there.
- Save your file as localinfo.

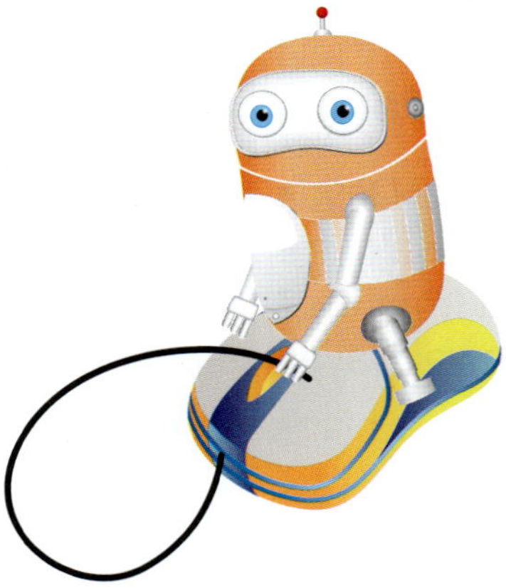

Challenge 2

- Search the Internet to find sites with information about Ancient Egypt.
- Copy the URLs of at least three relevant sites into your favourites folder.
- Save the URLs to an MS Word file along with images and useful information from the sites.

Challenge 3

- Which are the longest and highest mountain ranges for each continent?
- Use a search engine to find out.
- Search for images of these mountains.
- Find out about famous mountaineers.
- Copy some text and pictures to make an information sheet about mountains and their explorers.

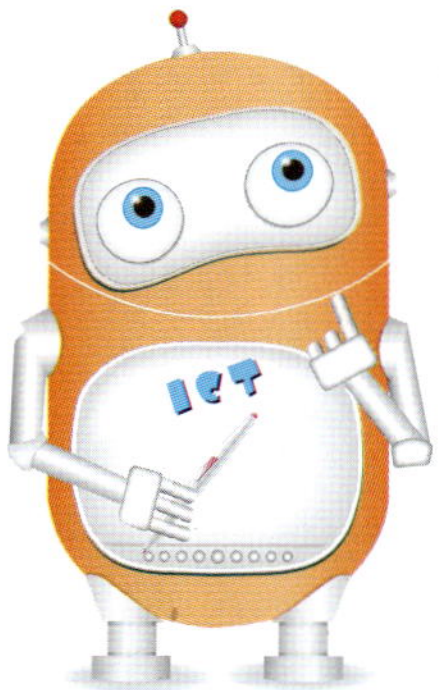

Module 7
Exploring Email

Learning Objectives

	Student is able to:	Pass/ Merit
1	Compose, edit, read and respond to emails	P
2	Add addresses to the address book	P
3	Use the address book to send copies, blind copies and forward emails	P
4	View an attachment	P
5	Add an attachment to an email	M
6	Manage email folders	M

7.1 Email account

Register a new account

- You will need an email account to complete this module.
- There are a few free email providers, e.g. Hotmail, Yahoo, etc.
- If you don't have an email account, ask your teacher to help you set up a new account with Hotmail.
- Each account needs a password. Think of one password that you can remember easily.
- Do not reveal your password to anybody.

Write your email address here:

____________________@hotmail.com

Composing new email

- Your class is doing a study on the most popular mode of transportation that the pupils use for coming to school.
- Compose an email to send to a friend.
- For practice purposes, your teacher will give each one of you a list of all the email addresses of your classmates.
- Look for your own email address and the email address of the classmate below you in the list.
- If you are the last one in the list, then look for the email address of the one at the top.
- Sign in to Hotmail. (You may need help from your teacher.)

- Click ⊕ New.
- In the space next to **To** type the email address of your classmate that you have just found.

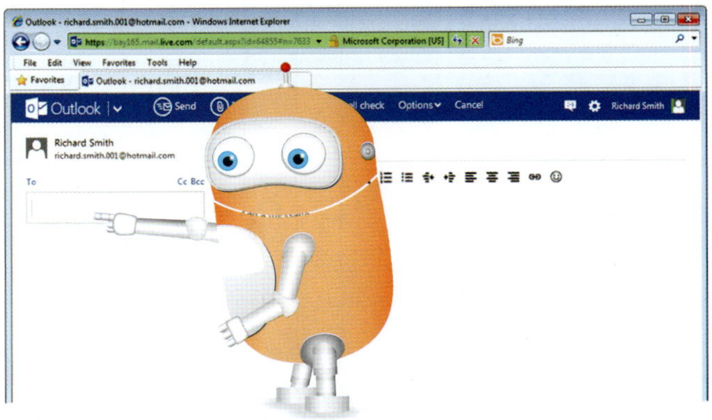

Subject

- Click on Add a subject and type: Transportation to school.
- Type your questionnaire in the space below Add a subject (do not make any changes).

  Dear xxx (type your friend's name),

  How are you?
  My class is doing a survey on what is the most popular transportation that we use to go to school. Can you tell me how do you go to school every day?

  A. By BUS B. By car C. By motorcycle D. By bicycle E. By van
  F. On foot G. Others

  Thanks.

  xxx (type your own name)

Editing

- Before you send out your email, you must always check for mistakes.
- You can also improve the content of the email.
- Look at the email you have just typed.
- Make the following changes:
  - Insert the word please after Can you ... in the second sentence.
  - Change By BUS to By bus.
  - Instead of just saying Thanks., change it to Thank you very much for your help.
- Select **Spell check** to do a spell check.

Send your email

- Click **Send** to send your email.
- A copy of your email is also saved in your Sent Folder.

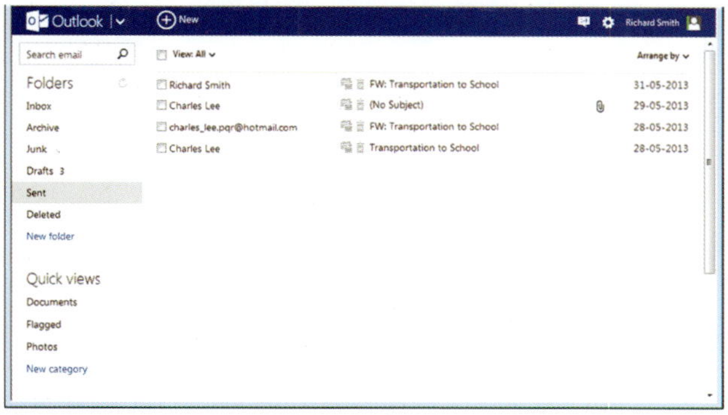

Receive email

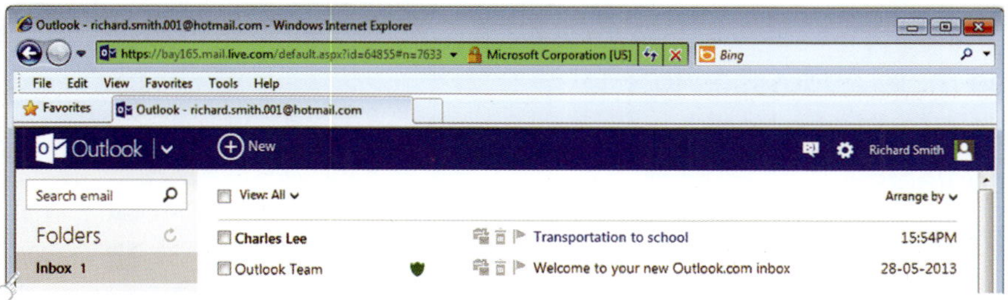

- Click **Inbox 1**.
- You should be receiving an email from your classmate (the one above you in the list) asking the same question about transportation.
- Click on the sender to open the email.

7.2 Replying to email

Replying to email

- Reply to the email that you have received.
- Click Reply.
- The recipient's email address box is filled with the sender's email address automatically.
- The subject is also filled automatically but with RE: added.
- Type your reply, and tell your friend how you go to school.
- Check your reply for any possible mistakes.
- Click Send to send out the email.

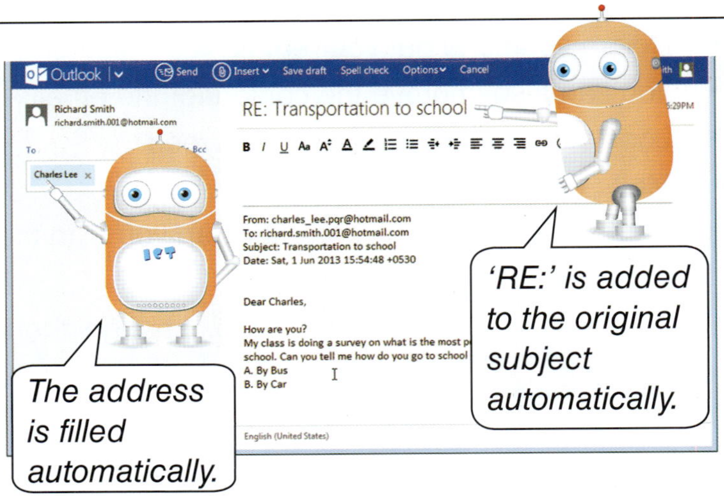

Contacts

- Set up an address book so that you can keep the email addresses of your friends.
- Click on ˅ next to Outlook on top left corner of the screen.
- A new menu will appear. Select People.
- Click New to add a new contact.
- Fill in the particulars of the new contact.
- Click Save to save the new contact.

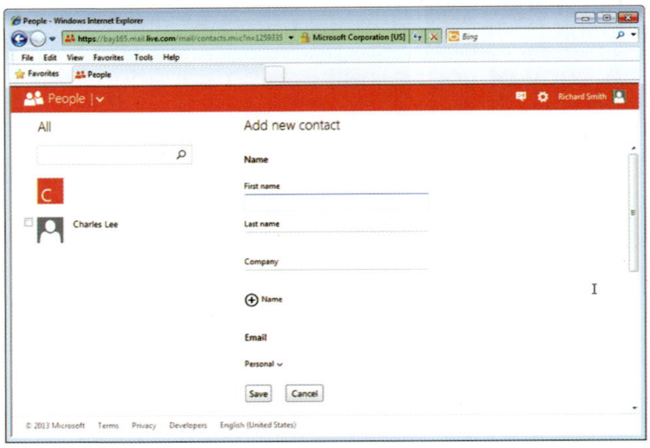

More contacts

- Do a snapshot of your list of contacts.
- Place it in a new document and save it as addressbook.docx.
- Add at least three more addresses to your list of contacts (address book).
- Save your new contacts.
- Do another snapshot of the address book.
- Place this second image below the first image in addressbook.docx to show that you know how to add new contacts.
- Save your document again.

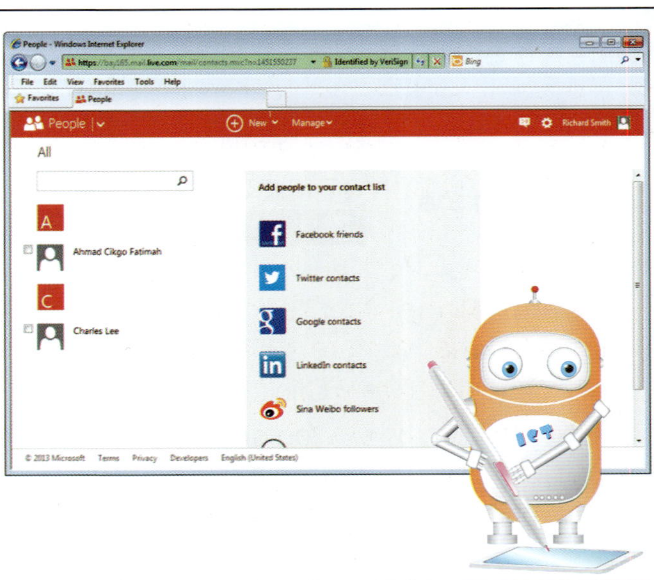

Forward

- Open the reply to the survey from your friend.
- Click Forward.
- Click To. You can select an address from the address book.
- Click on the name of your friend that you wish to send a copy to.
- 'FW:' is added to the original subject automatically.
- Click Send to send.

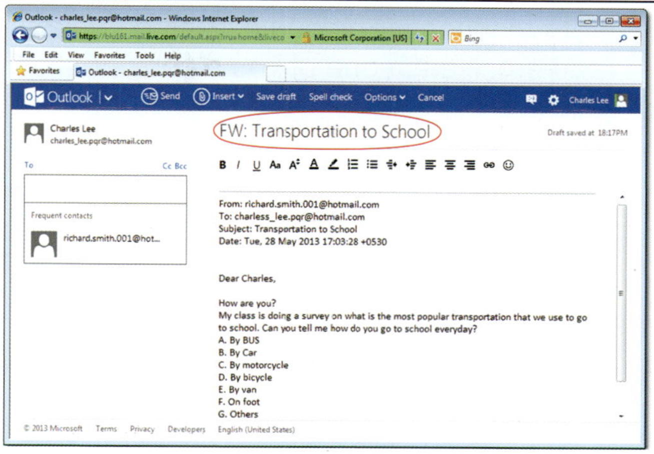

Sending copies: Cc

- Sometimes you need to send copies to different persons.
- This can be done easily by using the Cc feature.
- Open the reply to the survey from your friend again.
- Repeat the forward process in the last section to forward the email to a friend.
- Click Cc.
- Select an email address from the address book.
- Click Send to send.

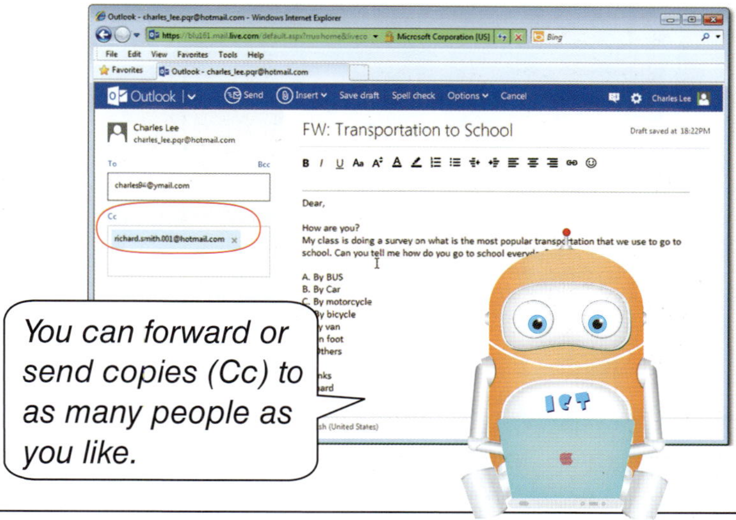

Blind copies: Bcc

- Repeat the last exercise.
- Before you send, click Bcc.
- Click the name of your teacher from the address book.
- This will send a blind copy to your teacher. All the other recipients will be unaware that you are sending the same copy to your teacher.
- Your teacher, however, will know who you are forwarding the email to and who you are sending copies to.

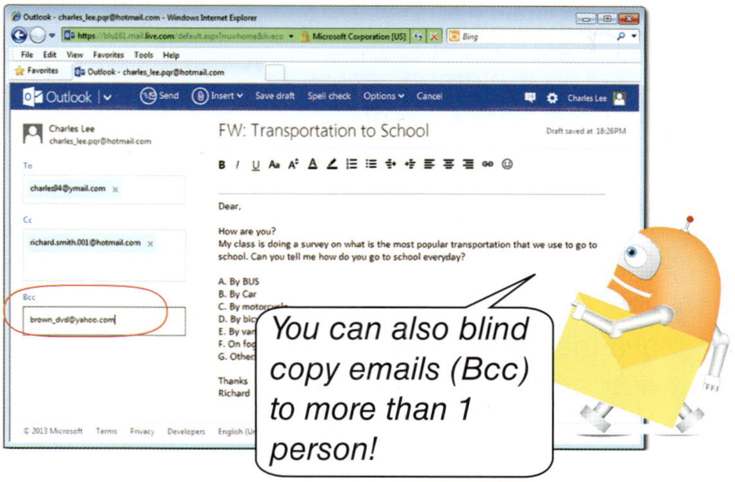

Save attachment

- Your teacher will help to collect the data and email each one of you a copy of the summary.
- Check your inbox for the email from your teacher.
- Click on the teacher's name (the sender) to open the email.
- Click,  to download the attached file or view it online.

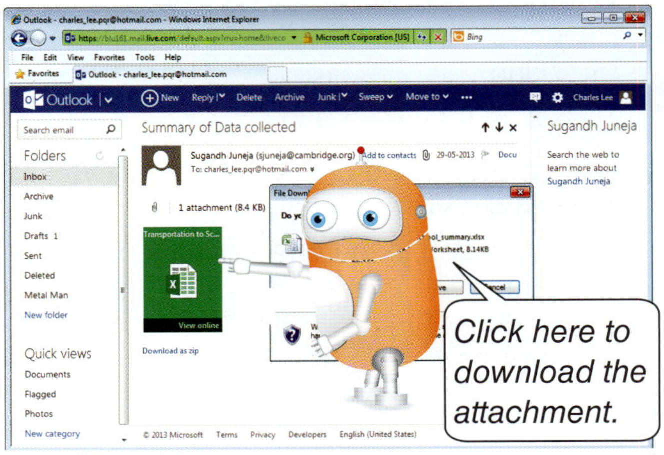

Download attached file

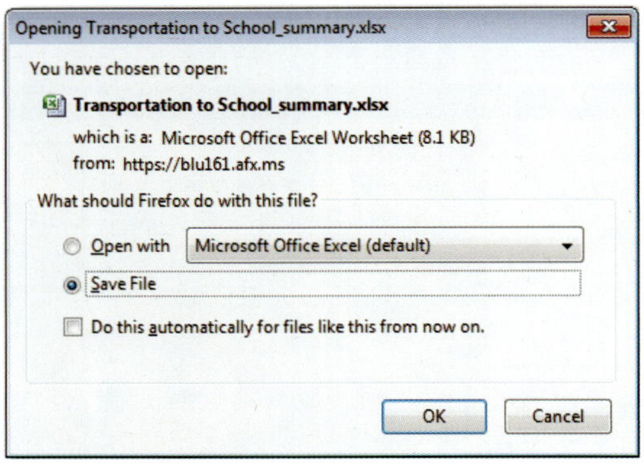

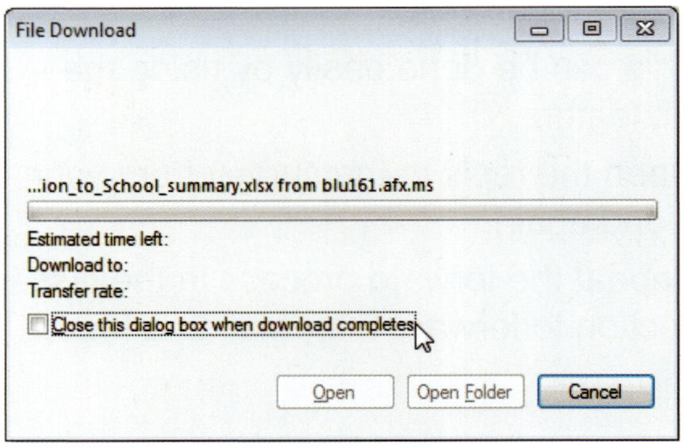

- Select Save to save the attached file in your usual folder.
- Click Close to open the window when the download is completed.

Open the attachment

- Open the attachment transportationtoschool using MS Excel.
- Based on the graph, answer the two questions under the graph.
- Save the completed worksheet as transp_graph.
- Do a screen snapshot of the graph and paste it into an MS Word document.
- Save the Word document as transportation with graph.

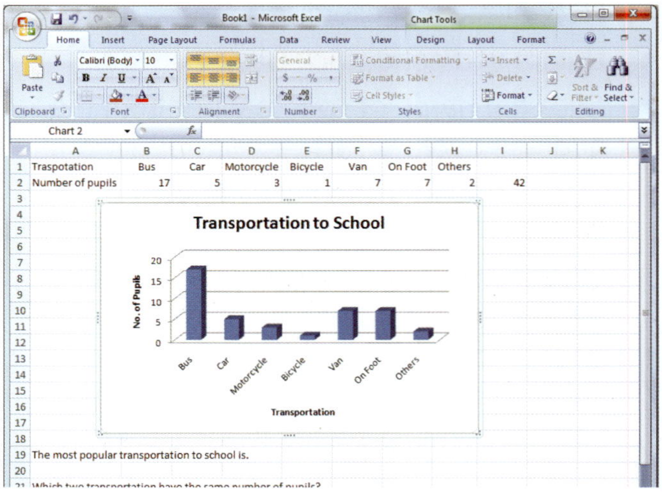

Preparing the email

- After you have completed the exercise, send the file back to your teacher for checking.
- Open the email with the file from your teacher.
- Click Reply.
- Type a simple reply email.
- You may use your own wording or you may type your email using the sample text given on the right.

Dear Mr/Ms xxx (your teacher's name),

I have completed the exercise as required. I hereby attach the file transp_graph for you to check, please.

Thank you.

Yours sincerely

XXX (your name)

Attachment

- Click Insert and select Files as attachments.
- Locate the file transp_graph that you have saved.
- Click Open.

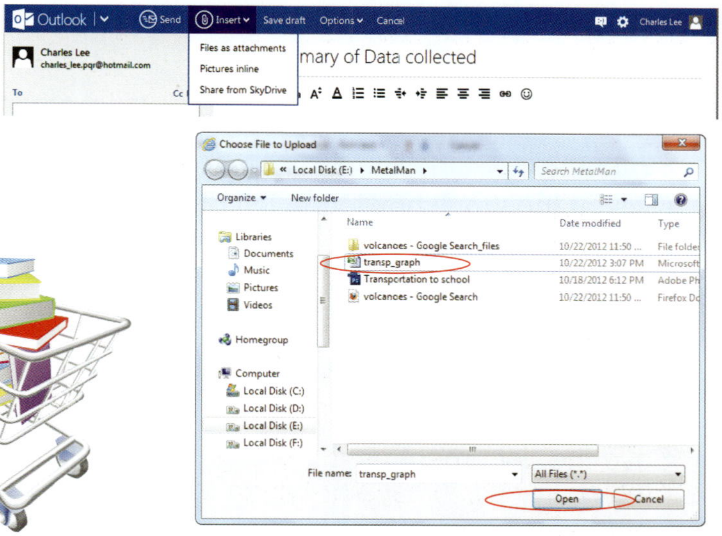

Sending the email

- Make sure that you see the attachment is indicated just below the subject of the email.

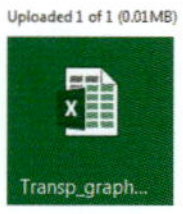

- Click to send out the email with the attachment.

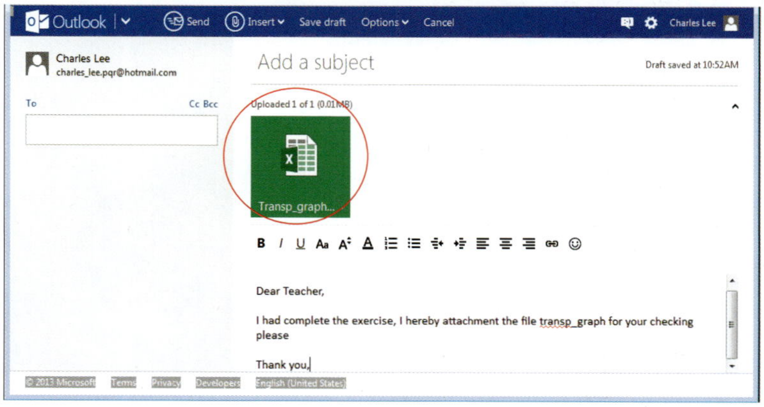

7.4 Managing folders

Learning Objective: 6

Creating a new folder

- Click Folders.
- Select New folder.
- Type your name as the name of the new folder.
- The new folder is indicated on the left-hand side of the window.

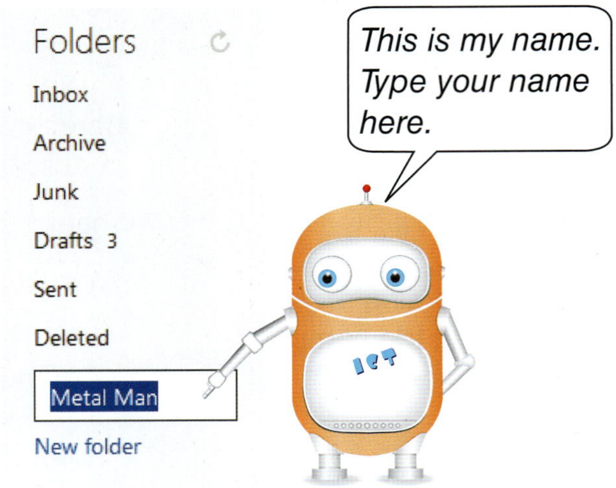

Move email to other folder

- Click Sent to open the sent emails.
- Click at the small box to the left of the recipient's name.
- Click Move to.
- Select your folder.
- Do a snapshot and place it as a new MS Word document.
- Save the document as managing folder.
- Print a copy and glue it in the space below.

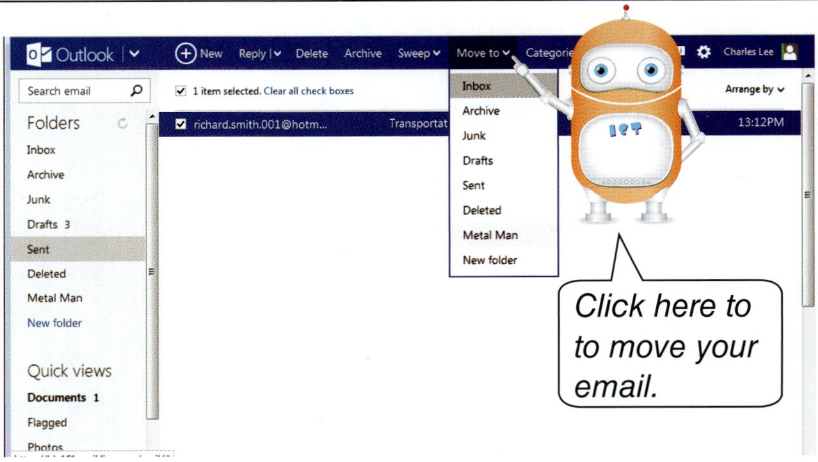

Optional extension and challenge activities

Module 7 – Exploring Email

Challenge 1

- Send an email to your teacher to tell her what you most enjoy about using a computer.
- Send a copy to yourself.
- Keep a copy of your email in a folder on the computer.

Challenge 2

- Download a recipe you like from the Internet and save it to an MS Word document.
- Send an email to a friend with the recipe as an attachment.

Challenge 3

- Send an email to a friend telling them about some work you have done with spreadsheets.
- Attach a spreadsheet to the email to show what you have learned.
- Copy your teacher into the email.

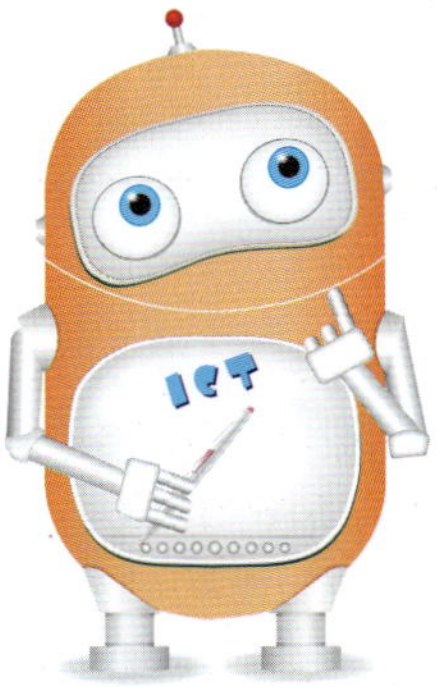

Module 8
Exploring Multimedia

Learning Objectives

	Student is able to:	Pass/ Merit
1	Create a page of text, images and sounds which are activated by appropriately named and positioned buttons	P
2	Use effective page design	P
3	Organise screens and identify appropriate choices and links	P
4	Create pages which offer the user options	M
5	Demonstrate how the presentation meets the needs of the intended audience	M

8.1 Learning about multimedia

What is multimedia?

- Multimedia presentations are computer-controlled ways of showing a lot of information.
- They can include:
  - text
  - photographs
  - drawings
  - paintings
  - videos
  - animations
  - sounds.

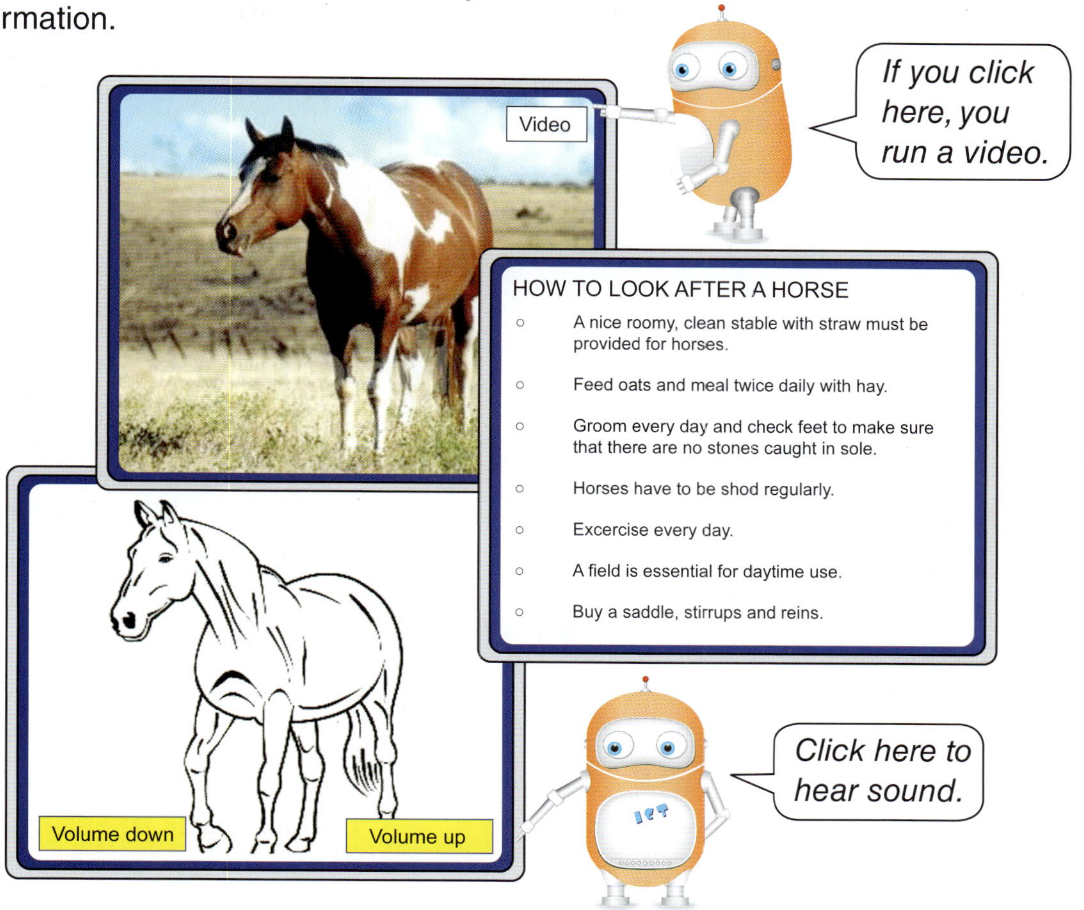

Slide shows

- Slide shows are multimedia presentations, like a TV programme.
- You can't choose what you see next. If you click the mouse, a new slide comes up.
- If you don't click the mouse, you will see a new slide after a few seconds.

A slide show can be a series of photos, sound clips and writing about a wedding or a celebration.

Interactive presentations

- Other presentations let you choose what information you see. These are called interactive presentations.
- You click the buttons to choose what to see or hear next.

8.2 MS PowerPoint

Learning Objective: 1

Make your first slide

- Click to open Start menu.
- Click ▶ All Programs.
- Click Microsoft Office PowerPoint 2007.

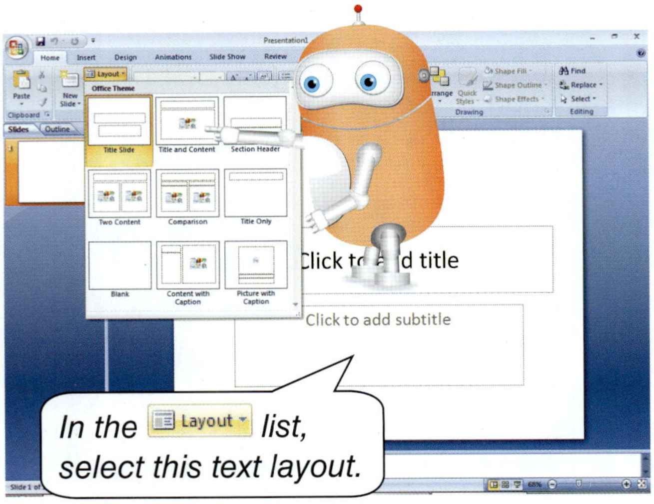

Add a title

- Click on the title.
- Type My Top 5 Songs.

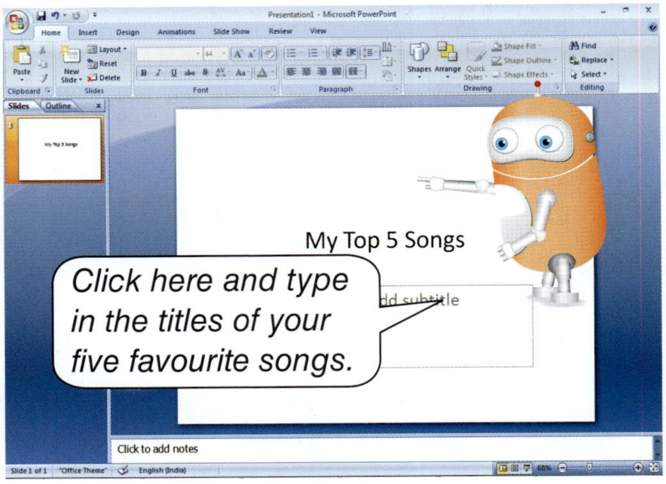

- Put each song title on a separate line.
- Start with the songs that you like best.

Numbers and bullets

- Select all the text in your list.
- Click to change the bullets to numbers.
- Click to change them back to bullets.

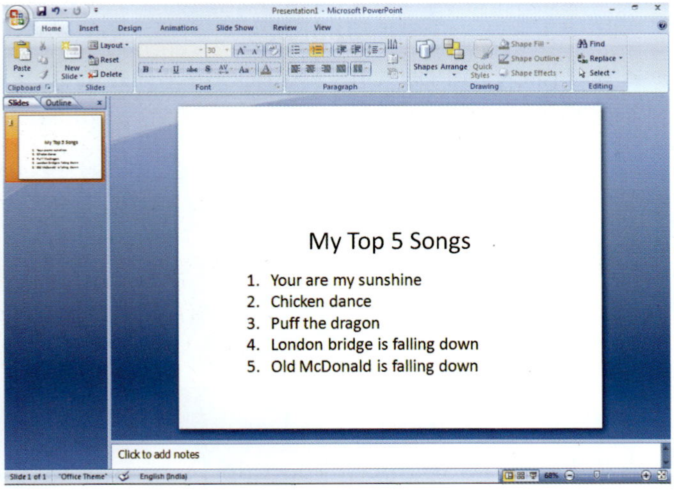

Save your presentation

- Click and select Save.
- In the File name: box, type a name for your file (e.g. My Top 5 Songs).
- Click Save.

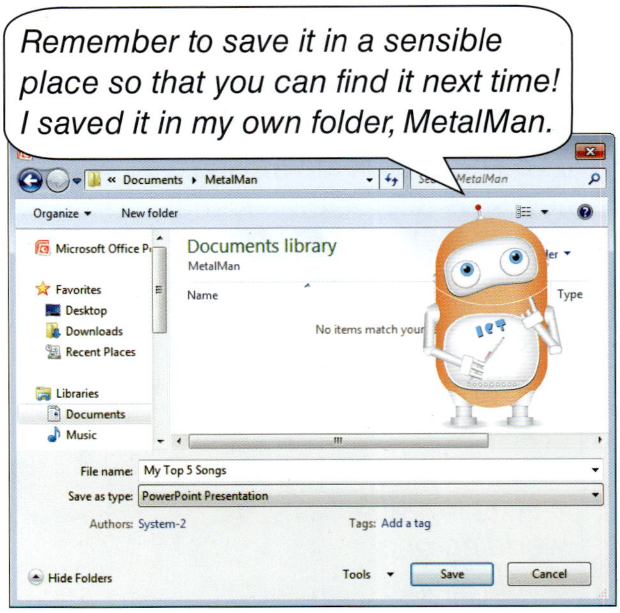

Layers

- Each graphic, for example a picture. a drawing, a shape or a block of text, is on a separate layer. You can see the top layers in front of the others.

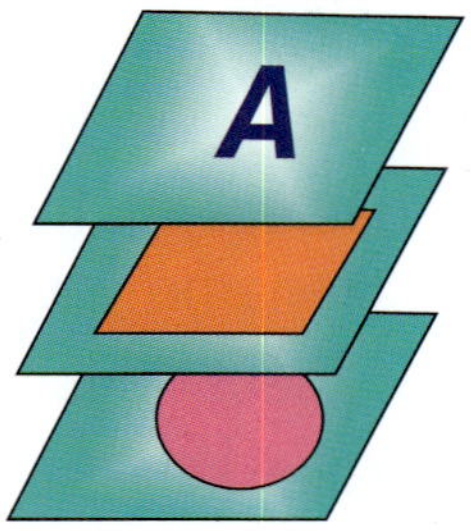

In this slide, the text is in the top layer. The rectangle is in the middle layer and the circle is in the bottom layer.

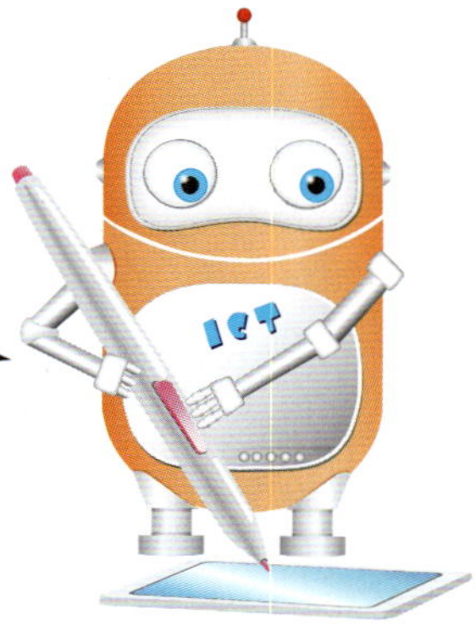

Open your presentation

- Click [Office button] to open Office menu.
- Click Open.
- Select My Top 5 Songs (or whatever filename you have used to save it).
- Click Open.

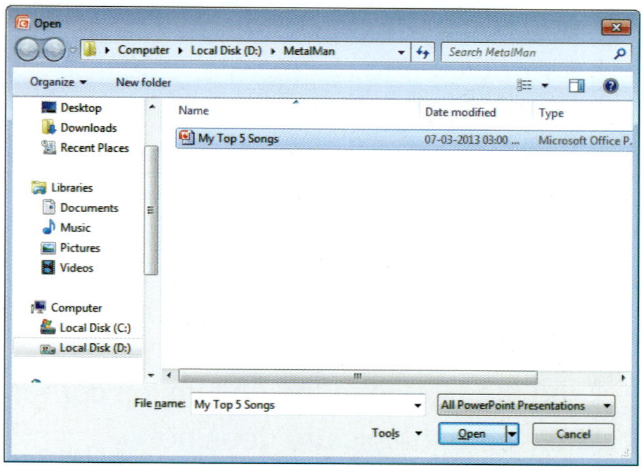

Add graphics

- Click on Insert tab then Shapes and select rectangle. The ↖ changes to +.
- Drag + to make a rectangle on your slide.
- On the Format tab, click Shape Outline to change the colour and thickness of the line.
- Click on Shape Fill choose a colour for the rectangle.
- Click on your rectangle and drag it so it is over the title of your slide.
- On the Format tab, click Send to Back.

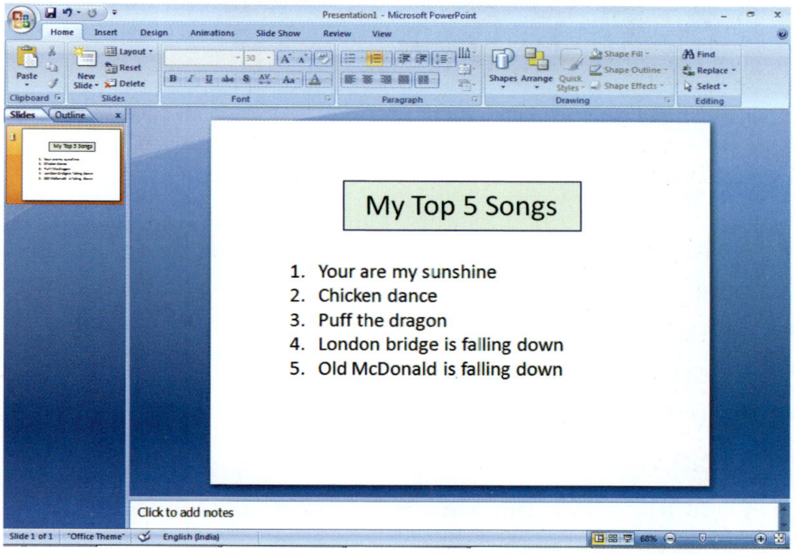

This puts the rectangle behind the text.

8.3 Adding pictures

Picture formats

- Pictures are saved in different formats. Look for these three types of file extension: .jpg .gif .png.
- If you use the Paint program to paint your own picture, the picture is normally saved as a .png graphic.

.jpg is commonly used for photos and .gif for simple diagrams.

Adding pictures

- Click on Insert tab.
- Click 

.
- Select My Top 5 Songs (or whatever filename you have used to save it).
- Select singing1.jpg.
- Click 

.

Resize the picture

- Drag one of the corners diagonally to reduce the size of the picture inserted.
- Drag the picture to the bottom left corner of the slide.
- Make sure the picture does not cover any of the text above.

Drag diagonally to reduce its size.

More pictures

- Insert one more picture, singing2.jpg, at the position shown.
- Adjust its size.
- Insert the next picture, singing3.jpg.
- Adjust it to a suitable size as shown.
- Click on Format tab .
- Click the arrow beside 

to see and choose 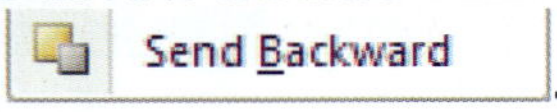

.
- This should put singing3.jpg behind singing2.jpg.
- To see how your slide looks, click on View tab.
- Click 

.
- Click  to save your slide.

Adding sounds

- Open the presentation slide My Top 5 Songs again.
- Click on Insert tab.
- Click Sound.
- Click Sound from File... .
- Select applause.wav or any other sound file given by your teacher.

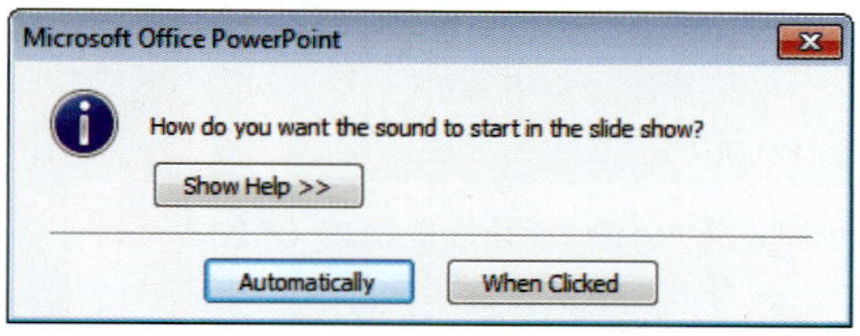

- Click Automatically.
- Click Open to play the sound automatically when the slide comes up.

Sound from Clip Organiser

- You can also insert a sound clip from the Clip Organiser.
- Click on Insert tab.
- Click Sound.
- Click Sound from Clip Organizer... .
- Scroll down the list to look at the different sound clips.

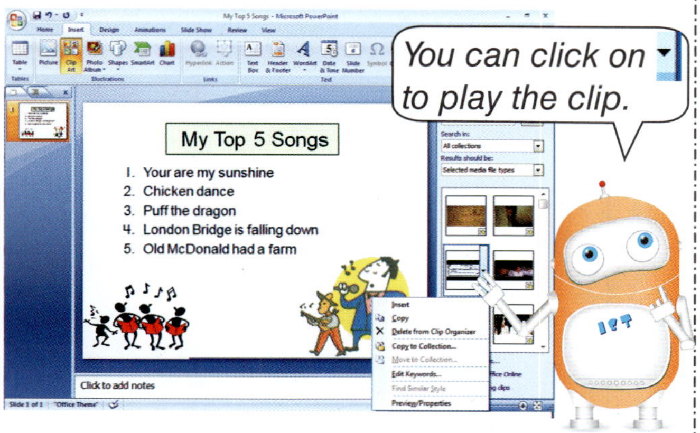

- When you click on the chosen sound you get a dialogue box.

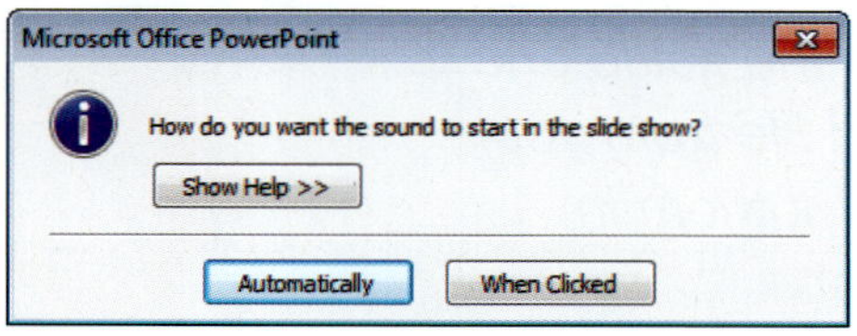

- Click to choose whether the sound is to be played automatically or when the icon is clicked on screen. A sound icon will appear on your slide.

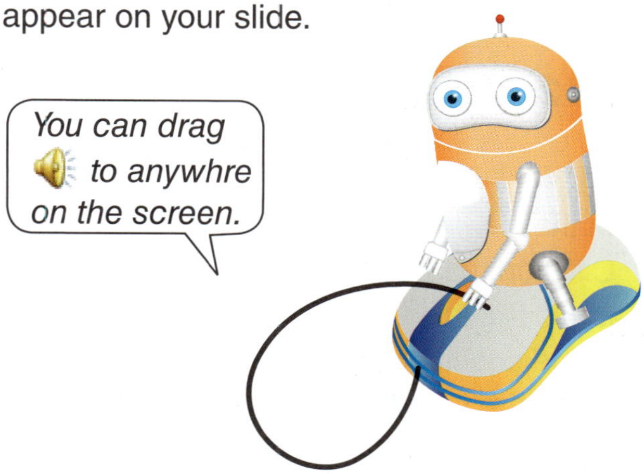

- Double-click on the sound icon to see Sound options tab. Hear the sound by clicking on Preview Play.
- Click Slide Show Volume to alter the volume of the sound.
- Click on the Home tab and select the text box icon.
- Click below the speaker icon.
- Type Click me to listen to the sound.
- Click Save to save your presentation.

8.5 Linear storyboards

Linear storyboard

- When slides come up one after the other in sequence, we call the presentation a linear storyboard.
- To plan a linear storyboard, draw a series of boxes on a piece of paper. In each box, write a short description of what will be on the slide.

Slide 1: Title

- Click  and select New.
- Double-click on Blank Presentation.
- In the Layout list, select the Title Only slide.

Books have covers that tell you what the book is about. A multimedia presentation has a title slide that tells you what it's about.

- Click in the text box and type How to make a cup of tea.
- Insert the picture tea.jpg below the title.

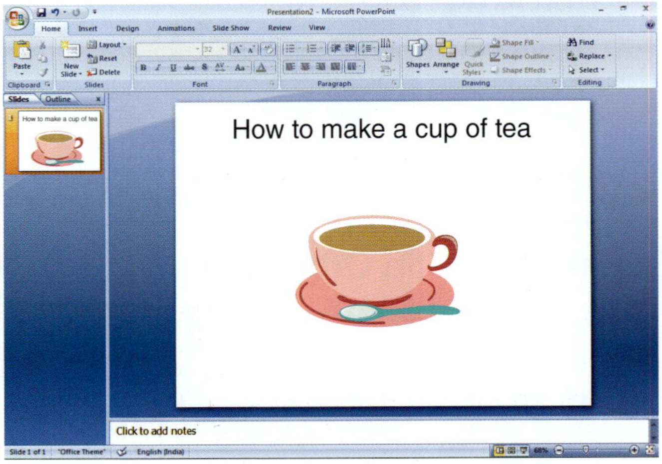

Slide 2: Step 1

- On the Home tab, click the arrow beside New Slide.
- In the New Slide list, select the Title Slide.
- Click on the title and type Step 1.
- Move the title box to the top.
- In the subtitle box, type Boil some water.
- Move the subtitle box to the top, below the title.
- Insert the picture kettle.gif below the subtitle. Adjust it to a suitable size. Insert the sound file kettlewhistle.wav.
- Click Automatically to play the sound automatically when the slide comes up.
- Click and select the speaker icon.
- Move the speaker icon to the bottom below the kettle.
- The icon must be visible for this exercise so as to provide evidence for inserting the sound clip.

Get the animated picture of the kettle and the sound file from your teacher. Put them in your folder.

Slide 3: Step 2

- On the Home tab, click the arrow beside New Slide.
- In the New Slide list, select Title Slide.
- Click on the title and type Step 2.
- Move the title box to the top.
- In the subtitle box, type Put the tea bag in the cup.
- Move the subtitle box to the top, below the title.
- Insert the picture emptycup.jpg.
- Insert another picture teabag.jpg.
- Position the teabag on top of the cup so that it looks as though the tea bag is dropping into the cup.

Slide 4: Step 3

- On the Home tab, click the arrow beside New Slide.
- In the New Slide list, select Title Slide.
- Click on the title and type Step 3.
- Move the title box to the top.
- In the subtitle box, type Pour the water in the cup.
- Move the subtitle box to the top, below the title.
- Insert the picture pouringwater.gif below the subtitle.
- Insert the sound clip pourwater.wav.
- Place the speaker icon at the bottom below the picture.

Slide 5: Step 4

- On the Home tab, click the arrow beside New Slide.
- In the New Slide list, select Title Slide.
- Click on the title and type Step 4.
- Move the title box to the top.
- In the subtitle box, type Stir the tea and leave it for 2 minutes.
- Move the subtitle boxes to the top, below the title.
- Insert the picture stirtea.jpg below the subtitle.
- Insert the sound file stircup.wav and place the speaker icon at the bottom below the cup.

Slide 6: Step 5

- On the Home tab, click the arrow beside New Slide.
- In the New Slide list, select Title Slide.
- Click on the title and type Step 5.
- Move the title box to the top.
- In the subtitle box, type Add sugar and/or milk.
- Move the subtitle box to the top, below the title.
- Insert the picture sugarmilk.jpg.

Slide 7: Enjoy your tea!

- On the Home tab, click the arrow beside New Slide.
- In the New Slide list, select Title Slide.
- Click on the title and type Enjoy your tea!
- Move the title and subtitle boxes to the top.
- Insert the picture teaready.gif below the title.
- Insert the sound clip drinktea.wav.
- Place the speaker icon below the picture.
- Adjust it to a suitable size.
- Click [save icon] to save your presentation as How to make a cup of tea.

Moving between your slides

- View the first slide.

> *Any object in your presentation that does an action when you click it is called a hotspot.*

- Click on Insert tab and select Shapes tool.
- Click Action Buttons.
- Select the button that points to the right.
- Click on the right bottom corner of the first slide. Drag to draw a small button.
- In the Action Settings dialogue window, select Mouse Click.
- Select Hyperlink to: button.
- Select Hyperlink to: box, click select Next Slide and click OK.

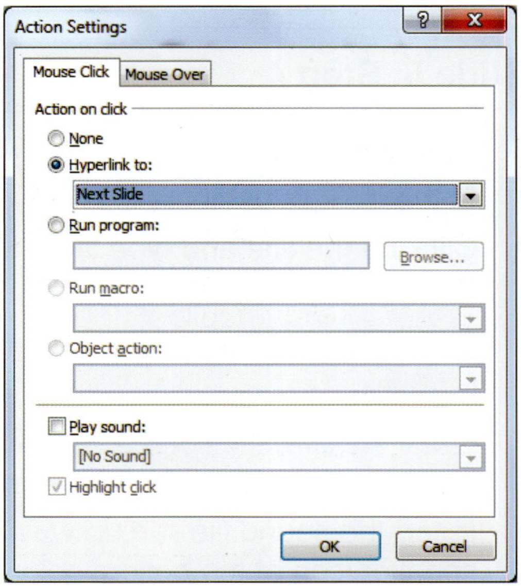

Going back

- View the next slide.
- Click **Action Buttons**.
- Select .
- Drag to draw the button at the left bottom corner of the slide.
- In the Action Settings dialogue window, select Mouse Click.
- Select Hyperlink to: button .
- Select Hyperlink to: box, click .
- Select Previous Slide and click OK.
- Copy action button and paste it in the right-hand bottom corner of the slide.
- Paste the same action button in the right-hand bottom corner of slides 3, 4, 5 and 6.
- Copy and paste it in the left-hand bottom corner of slides 3, 4, 5, 6 and 7.
- Do not paste on the last slide.
- Do not paste on the first slide.
- Use the textbox tool to insert a text box below .
- Type Next.
- Use the textbox tool to insert a text box below .
- Type Previous.
- Copy these two text boxes to all the other slides.

Slide show

- To view the slide show, click on View tab.
- Click Slide Show.
- You can also click the icon.
- Another way is to simply tap F5.
- Tapping Esc at any time during the show will terminate the slide show and return to the edit mode of PowerPoint.
- Use one of the above methods to view your presentation.
- As you watch the presentation, check for spelling mistakes and the layout of the presentation.
- When you are satisfied with the presentation, click to save it again.

Review

- Study the presentation you have just created.
- Which of the following types of audience can we show the presentation to?
  - ▫ Kids from kindergarten
  - ▫ Secondary pupils
  - ▫ Working adults
  - ▫ Tourists
- What was the purpose of inserting the pictures?

  ____

  ____

- Which do you prefer, static pictures or animated pictures? Why?

  ____

  ____

  ____

- Do you think adding sound effects makes the presentation more interesting and appealing to the audience?

  ____

Complex tree storyboard

When we don't link slides in a fixed order, we call this a complex tree presentation. In complex tree presentations, you can link each slide to more than one slide.

- Create a storyboard on paper for your complex tree presentation.
- Draw a box for each slide.
- Write the headings you will put on each slide.
- Draw an arrow from each box to show the links between the slides.

National Parks

- Your school Geography Club has requested that you help to prepare a presentation on the National Parks of Sarawak, the largest state in Malaysia.
- They would like to see some photos of each of the National Parks and any other relevant graphics like logos.
- Each National Park must also have a description of it.

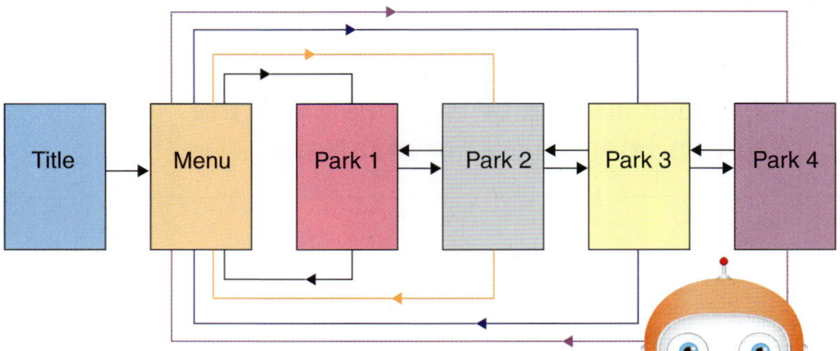

You may need more boxes for this project.

National Parks presentation

- Click [Office button] and select New.
- Double-click on Blank Presentation.
- In the Layout list, select Title Only.
- Click on Design tab.
- In the Themes group, scroll down the side scroll bar.
- Select a background from the list displayed.
- Click in the text box and type:

  National Parks of Sarawak,
  The largest state in Malaysia.

I selected the paper.pot slide design. Do you like it?

Learning Objectives: 1, 2

Main menu

- Insert a new slide.
- Use the **Title Only** slide layout.
- Type Main Menu as the title.
- Insert the map of Sarawak sarawakmap.jpg.
- Follow the positions of National Parks as seen on the right, type the names using textbox: Tanjung Datu, Bako, Niah, Gunung Mulu, Batang Ai.
- Use textbox to add an instruction below the map:

  Click at each of the names to see a brief description.

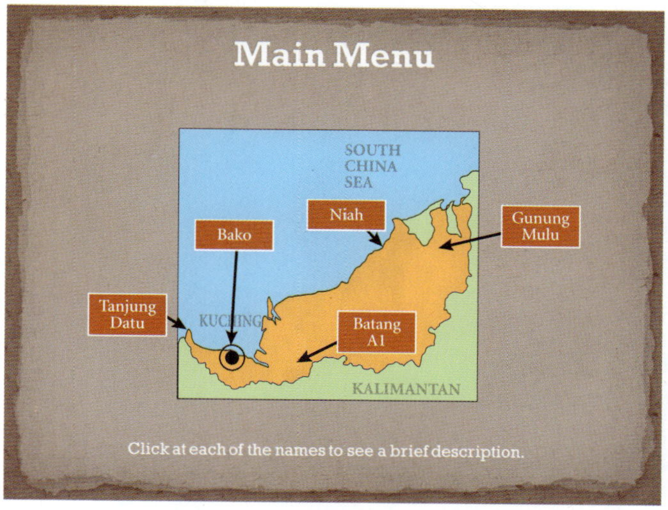

Description of each slide

- Create a slide to describe each of the National Parks of Sarawak.
- You can follow the sample slide given or use your own creativity to produce the slide based on the information and graphics given.
- Insert a new slide.
- Use the **Title and Content** slide layout.
- Type Tanjung Datu as the title.
- Insert the logo of the park, LogoTD.jpg and place it next to the title.
- Insert the photo Tg-Datu.jpg, and resize it to the appropriate size as shown in the completed sample slide.
- Insert another photo, TanjungDatu.jpg, resize it and place it on top of the first photo.
- Arrange the two photos as shown.
- Insert a textbox and type the description.
- Place it below the photos.

Tg-Datu.jpg

LogoTD.jpg

Completed slide

TanjungDatu.jpg

Mountains sweep down to the sea in this park on the extreme western tip of the State. The debris-free mountain streams ensure crystal-clear waters off some of Sarawak's finest beaches. There are also coral formations close in shore that make this as-yet unexplored dive site ideal for scuba diving. On shore the park is rich in flora and fauna.

To put a photo behind another photo, first select the photo, click on Format tab, select Send to Back, *select* Send to Back.

Bako

Bako1.jpg

Bako2.jpg

Logobako.jpg

Bako3.jpg

- Based on the sample slide shown above, create a slide to describe the Bako National Park.

Just a short ride from Kuching, Sarawak's oldest national park is home to the rare proboscis monkey. It is an ideal introduction to what the State has to offer.

Niah

Niah1.jpg

Niah2.jpg

Logoniah.jpg

Niah3.jpg

- Based on the slide above, create one new slide for Niah National Park.

Humans inhabited the Niah Caves some 40,000 years ago. Among the Palaeolithic and Neolithic paintings and artefacts is Southeast Asia's oldest burial site, discovered in 1958. Today, local Penans climb flimsy bamboo scaffolds to collect birds' nests from the cave ceiling.

8.8 More slides

Learning Objectives: 1, 2

Gunung Mulu

Logomulu.jpg

Mulu2.jpg

Mulu1.jpg

Mulu3.jpg

- Based on the sample slide shown above, create a slide to describe the Gunung Mulu National Park.

A true tropical wonderland, Gunung Mulu has it all – the world's most extensive cave system, the world's largest cave chamber, limestone pinnacles, jungle trekking, rock climbing, kayaking and a chance to meet the nomadic Penans.

Batang Ai

Logobatangai.jpg

Batangai1.jpg

Batangai2.jpg

- Based on the slide above, create one new slide for Batang Ai National Park.

Enclosing a huge lake, the park is inhabited by wild orang-utans, gibbons and hornbills. There are also several traditional Iban longhouses. You can enjoy the wilderness while pampering yourselves with the comforts of the nearby Batang Ai Hilton Longhouse Resort.

8.9 Linking the slides

Learning Objective: 4

Hyperlinks

- View slide 2 Main Menu.
- Highlight the name Tanjung Datu.
- Click on Insert tab.
- Select Hyperlink.
- Select Place in This Document.
- Select 3. Tanjung Datu from the slide titles window.
- Click OK.
- Repeat to establish the links for all the other parks.

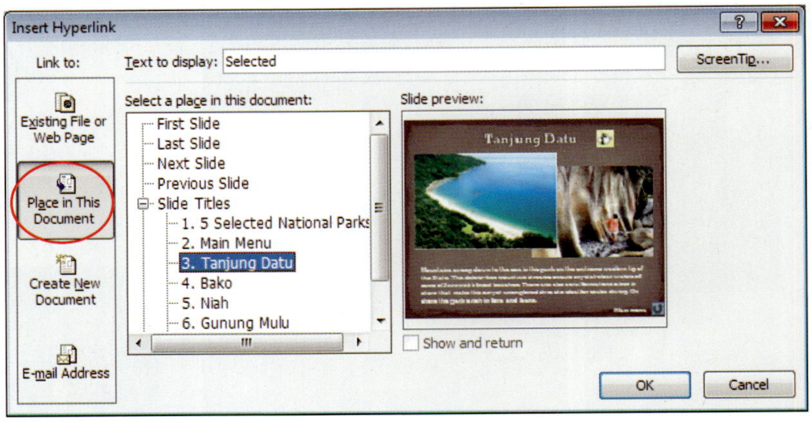

Create action buttons

- Go back to view slide 3 – Tanjung Datu.
- Click on Insert tab and select Shapes tool.
- Click Action Buttons.
- Select return.
- Draw the return icon at the bottom right corner.
- Use textbox to put the label Main Menu next to the return icon.
- Link it to the Main Menu slide.
- Copy the return icon and paste it onto slides 4 to 7.
- Link slides 4 to 7 to the Main Menu slide.

Put the return icon here.

Testing

- Click to save your presentation.
- Go back to view the first slide.
- Click to run the slide show.
- Run through the slide show slide by slide.
- Make sure all the hyperlinks from the names of the parks to each individual slide work.
- Make sure all the links associated with the return icon bring you back to the Main Menu.
- When you are satisfied with all your links, save your presentation again.

Once you establish a link, the link is indicated by the underline. If you point to the link, the mouse pointer will change its shape to . Click at each link to make sure that they are linked to the correct slide.

8.13 Self-evaluation

Learning Objective: 5

Evaluation

- The presentation of National Parks of Sarawak is targeted to the Geography Club members. Do you think that it has met the needs of the members?
- Run the presentation and evaluate the slides.
- What are the strong points or weaknesses of the slides?
- Look at the following features and comment:
  - Are the contents and instructions on the Main Menu clear to the audience?

    ____
  - Why do you think a map is provided on the Main Menu?

    ____
  - With the help of the map, do you think all the members know the location of each of the National Parks?

    ____
  - Are the maps useful in helping the audience to identify the National Parks better?

    ____
  - Why do you think we insert colourful photos?

    ____
  - Which do you prefer, colourful photos or just plain text?

    ____
  - Identify the weaknesses and suggest how they can be improved.

    ____

    ____

    ____

    ____

    ____

    ____

    ____

    ____

    ____

8.11 Project

More National Parks

- There are actually more than 5 National Parks in Sarawak.
- You will be given the related logos, photos and descriptions of each of the National Parks.
- First of all, add 4 more names on the main menu (refer to the map on the right for the locations): Similajau, Lambir Hills, Loagan Bunut and Kubah.
- Create a new slide for each of these four National Parks.
- You can choose any layout that you like.
- All the slides must be linked from the Main Menu and be able to return back to the Main Menu.

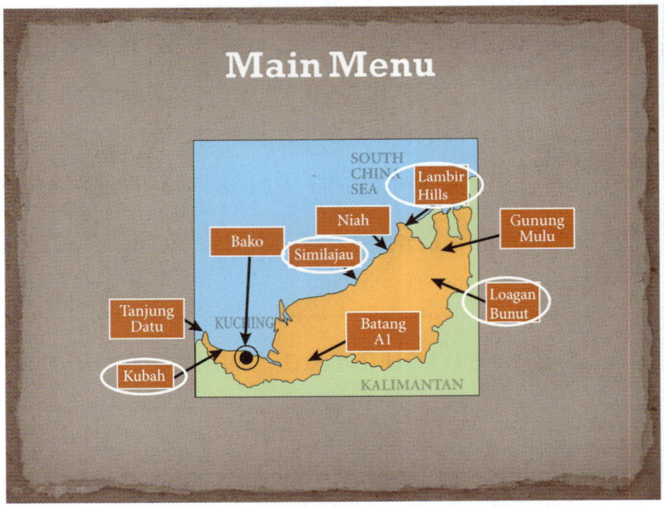

Similajau National Park

A combination of golden sandy beaches and rainforest make the park perfect for bird watching, bathing, trekking, coastal cruises and viewing the wildlife.

Logosimilajau.jpg

Similajau1.jpg

Similajau2.jpg

Similajau3.jpg

Similajau4.jpg

- Besides the logo, choose 2 or 3 photos fromthe list above.
- Arrange the photos, resized if necessary, so that they are not too crowded.
- Link back to the Main Menu.

Lambir Hills National Park

Logolambir.jpg

Lambir1.jpg

Lambir2.jpg

Lambir3.jpg

Lambir4.jpg

Now known to be the world's most bio-diverse forest, Lambir Hills is home to more than 1,000 species of tree. There are plants and insects here that have not yet been discovered as well as waterfalls and bathing pools for a quick dip.

- Besides the logo, choose 2 or 3 photos from the list above.
- Arrange the photos, resized if necessary, so that they are not too crowded.
- Link back to the Main Menu.

Loagan Bunut National Park

Logoloagan.jpg

Loagan1.jpg

Loagan2.jpg

Loagan3.jpg

Loagan4.jpg

The centrepiece of this park is a unique disappearing lake. Normally Loagan Bunut is a scenic lake, Sarawak's largest, but in the dry season it shrinks and disappears. It is an ideal spot for bird watchers and anyone interested in the culture of the Berawan people who inhabit the lake and have developed distinctive fishing practices.

- Besides the logo, choose 2 or 3 photos from the list above.
- Arrange the photos, resized if necessary, so that they are not too crowded.
- Link back to the Main Menu.

Kubah National Park

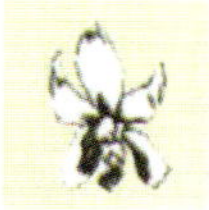
Logokubah.jpg

Kubah1.jpg

Kubah2.jpg

Kubah3.jpg

Kubah4.jpg

Just 20 km from Kuching, the capital city of Sarawak, Kubah's waterfalls, crystal-clear rivers and plant life make it a popular day trip for locals as well as visitors.

- Besides the logo, choose 2 or 3 photos from the list above.
- Arrange the photos, resized if necessary, so that they are not too crowded.
- Link back to the Main Menu.
- Save your presentation.
- Test your presentation to ensure that the slides are linked properly.

Optional extension and challenge activities

Module 8 – Exploring Multimedia

Challenge 1

- Use PowerPoint to create a presentation about your school to show to new pupils.
- Use photos, text and slide transitions to make it interesting.

Challenge 2

- Use PowerPoint to create a presentation about musical instruments.
- Download some sound files from the Internet and add them to the pages as audio buttons which can be clicked to hear the sound of the instrument.

Challenge 3

- Use PowerPoint to create a 4 screen presentation about safari animals.
- The first page should have buttons which link to the other three pages.
- Each of the linked pages should have a button to go back to the first page.